"This study is deep and packed with surprising insights! I enjoyed exploring the story of Hagar—an often-discarded woman who played a profound part in human history. I love how Shadia weaves in her personal experiences, helping readers connect with her and understand how to apply the teaching to their own lives. This study beautifully captures the depth of God's love for all people. I am excited to share it with others!

—**Francine Rivers,** international best-selling author

"This study is a personal and compelling guide to a powerful and underappreciated story of God's faithfulness."

—**Bible Study Magazine,** a publication of Faithlife, the creator of Logos Bible Software

"Few biblical stories illustrate hope in the hard places of life better than Hagar's. Shadia beautifully illuminates that hope, offering encouragement not only for the destination of our lives but also for the journey. Through this study, readers will be inspired to trust God, embrace His purposes, and experience His victory."

—**Chris Tiegreen,** author of the *Dancing in the Desert Devotional Bible* and various One Year devotionals

"This refreshing study digs deep into the life of Hagar. . . . Thought provoking and practical, it will help readers develop a desire to serve our Savior. I highly recommend it!"

—**Fouad Masri,** founder and president of Crescent Project

"*Hagar: Rediscovering the God Who Sees Me* is certain to inspire its readers to go deeper in understanding God's unfathomable love and purposes, specifically amid our personal heartaches and pain. . . . This extensive study draws us deeper into the biblical text to search for answers. There we find ourselves prompted by Shadia's own transparency to surface our intimate longings. Relating to Hagar as a person who was used, abused, and rejected brings us face-to-face with a God who reaches far beyond cultural expectations to meet Hagar in the midst of her pain. This study will lead you there as well."

—**Bev Hislop,** D.Min., author of *Shepherding a Woman's Heart* and professor emerita of Pastoral Care, Western Seminary, Portland, Oregon

"Hagar is sometimes downplayed as a minor and almost expendable figure in the more prominent story of Abraham and Sarah, but Shadia Hrichi's book reveals a complex and fascinating woman facing the same spiritual struggles as the rest of us. All of us have something to learn from this woman who suffered despair, rejection, and abuse but still managed to find hope in the One she called the 'God Who Sees Me.'"

—**Joseph Bentz,** author of *Nothing is Wasted*

"A Bible study on Sarah's Egyptian slave girl? I've never done a study on Hagar before, but Shadia reveals that there is more to Hagar's story than meets the eye. She was used and abandoned. Where was God in that? I've also wrestled with this question at times. Who hasn't? Thank you, Shadia, for opening my eyes to Hagar's story; in doing so, it helped me to see myself."

—**Kay Marshall Strom,** author and international speaker

HAGAR

Rediscovering the God Who Sees Me

Shadia Hrichi

LEAFWOOD
PUBLISHERS

an imprint of Abilene Christian University Press

HAGAR

Rediscovering the God Who Sees Me

L E A F W O O D
P U B L I S H E R S
an imprint of Abilene Christian University Press

Copyright © 2017 by Shadia Hrichi

ISBN 978-0-89112-470-2 | LCCN 2017028574

Printed in the United States of America

LIBRARY OF CONGRESS CATALOGING-IN-PUBLICATION DATA
Names: Hrichi, Shadia, 1967- author.
Title: Hagar : rediscovering the God who sees me / by Shadia Hrichi.
Description: Abilene, Texas : Leafwood Publishers, 2017. | Series: Behind the
    seen: exploring the Bible's unsung heroes
Identifiers: LCCN 2017028574 | ISBN 9780891124702 (pbk.)
Subjects: LCSH: Hagar (Biblical figure)—Textbooks.
Classification: LCC BS580.H24 H75 2017 | DDC 222/.11092—dc23
LC record available at https://lccn.loc.gov/2017028574

Cover design by Thinkpen Design
Interior text design by Sandy Armstrong, Strong Design

Leafwood Publishers is an imprint of Abilene Christian University Press
ACU Box 29138, Abilene, Texas 79699

1-877-816-4455 | www.leafwoodpublishers.com

22 23 24 25 26 27 / 7 6 5 4 3

CONTENTS

ACKNOWLEDGMENTS

THROUGHOUT EACH OF OUR LIVES, GOD PLACES MANY people on our path as He forms and fashions us for His wonderful purposes. To express my gratitude to each one would be quite an endeavor; nevertheless, I wish to give special recognition to those who specifically helped bring this study to fruition.

To all of God's servants at Leafwood Publishers and ACU Press: thank you for believing in me, for your excitement and enthusiasm for this work, for your commitment to excellence every step of the way, and most especially, for the humble privilege of serving alongside a group of people who follow Christ's example of kindness, humility, and love.

To my marvelous group of test readers, Sandi Miller, Linda Dunning, Jackie Kupitz, Kendra Burrows, and Dawna Hetzler: how could I ever thank you for the countless hours you have given to work through this study and provide such invaluable feedback? Your efforts have genuinely enhanced this study. Your sacrifice means more to me than you can know.

To Francine Rivers: when God allowed us to cross paths several years ago, I could never have imagined the blessing He would orchestrate through your ongoing encouragement and enthusiasm for this study. Thank you, Francine; you have blessed my heart!

To Joseph Bentz, Kay Marshall Strom, and Chris Tiegreen: thank you for reviewing the early manuscript, encouraging me to seek publication, and for endorsing the final work.

To Fouad Masri, Bev Hislop, and Mark Matta: I am truly grateful to each of you for your kind words, confidence, and endorsement of this work.

To Kathy Ide, Judith Robl, and Jan Kern: thank you for your superb editing and mentorship during the early stages of this project.

To the wonderful leadership and all the saints at Venture Christian Church: thank you for all of the ways you have invested in this ministry through your love, prayers, and gifts. I am especially thankful to you for cheering me on when I struggle to press onward. I am deeply humbled to be a part of such a godly, generous, and loving church family.

To many family and friends who have offered their love and support in more ways that I can count, including Dana Christensen who opened the door to her lovely mountain retreat in order to provide me with a pleasant haven for extended times of writing: thank you! I am also grateful to Kendra Burrows, Hope Hickey Netterville, and Karen Mutsch for their help in formatting the extensive bibliography.

And of course, there would be no study, no ministry, and nothing of value for me to offer apart from the saving grace of my Lord and Savior, Jesus Christ, who gave His all for me. Thank you, Jesus, for opening my eyes to Your boundless mercy, grace, and love. May Your name—Yours alone—be glorified.

ABOUT THE AUTHOR

 **SHADIA HRICHI IS A PASSIONATE BIBLE** teacher, author, and speaker who has a heart for seeing lives transformed by the power of God's Word. Having experienced much heartache, such as a broken home, abortion, and divorce, Shadia captures the hearts of her audience as she illustrates God's love, faithfulness, and power of redemption through her personal experiences.

She has received a master's in biblical and theological studies from Western Seminary, as well as a master's in criminal justice from the State University of New York. Shadia is the author of several books, including *Legion: Rediscovering the God Who Rescues Me*, the second study in her Behind the Seen series, and *Worthy of Love*, a story-driven Bible study for post-abortion healing. In addition to teaching Bible studies, Shadia is often invited to speak at churches, conferences, and other events. Her insightful, witty, yet vulnerable teaching style reveals a compassion for the hurting, love for Jesus, and uncompromising commitment to the truth of God's Word.

Residing in northern California, Shadia is an active member of Venture Christian Church and loves visiting the ocean each week for "a date with Jesus." Be sure to visit www.shadiahrichi.com and sign up for updates to be among the first to find out about Shadia's next study.

ABOUT THE STUDY

WELCOME! I AM THRILLED THAT YOU DESIRE TO JOURNEY with me in *Rediscovering the God Who Sees Me!* God has so much to teach us through Hagar's story, and I can hardly wait for us to get started.

This book is divided into seven weeks, each comprised of five days of personal study. Each day includes one or more questions suitable for group discussion. These questions are followed by a ⌘. Be sure not to overlook these questions even if you are working through the material on your own. There are also Pause to Ponder sections throughout the study. These are designed to provide you with a time of personal reflection. Use the space in the margins (or if you prefer, a journal or notebook) to respond to these questions. For readers desiring to dig even deeper, I've prepared extra questions, which are preceded by a ✐.

Each day of study will take approximately 45 minutes. If you have time to go deeper, consider integrating the extra questions into your study time. At the end of each day, there is a Your Turn section for personal application. These are very important. While studying our Bibles can stir our hearts and open our eyes to wonderful truths, only when we apply what we have learned will it have a lasting impact for God's kingdom. In addition to this workbook, optional video teaching sessions are available at www.shadiahrichi.com/hagar.

During my study of Hagar, I often found myself fascinated by secondary topics related to the material. As such, I included a supplemental reading for each week. While they are not essential for the study, you may find them enjoyable and informative.

Before you begin, take a few moments to ask the Holy Spirit to guide you over the next seven weeks and to bless your commitment to this study. Then, as you open your Bible and your heart, begin each day with an eager expectation of *Rediscovering the God Who Sees Me.*

GROUP STUDY TIPS

BECAUSE ANY DEEP WORK OF GOD REQUIRES A SACRIFICE of time spent in His Word and in His presence, the volume of material in an in-depth study can be challenging for some participants. For this reason, several suggestions are provided to help you facilitate the study when participants have varying levels of time constraints.

Video Teaching Sessions

Eight optional video teaching sessions to enhance and serve as a complement to this study are available at https://www.shadiahrichi.com/hagar. To integrate these videos into your study, watch the Introductory Session before you begin. Then, watch Sessions One through Seven after completing each of those weeks in the study. The Introductory Session is sixteen minutes long; Sessions One through Seven are twenty to twenty-five minutes long.

Plan an Extended Schedule

Rather than meeting for seven weeks, allow two weeks for each chapter, for a total of fourteen weeks. Every other week, invite participants to watch Shadia's video teaching sessions. These modifications will also provide periodic opportunities for participants to "catch up" on anything they may have missed or to spend extra time on areas of the study they many wish to explore further.

Customized Commitments for a Seven-Week Schedule

Based on a seven-week format, the following are suggested assignments based on an individual's time constraints.

For All Participants

- Read through each day's material, including the assigned Bible passages.
- Optional: read the Supplemental Reading section as provided in various weeks.

Light (15 minutes a day)

- Complete the Your Turn personal application section at the end of each day.
- If you have time, complete the Group Discussion questions identified with a ◌⸲⸲⸲∼.

Moderate (30 minutes a day)

- Complete the various Pause to Ponder personal reflection sections as well as the Your Turn personal application section at the end of each day.
- Complete the Group Discussion questions identified with a ◌⸲⸲⸲∼.

In-Depth (45 minutes a day)

- Complete all questions except for the Extra questions identified with a ◌∼.

All-In (60 minutes a day)

- Complete all of the questions, including the Extra questions identified with a ◌∼.
- Read all the Supplemental Reading sections.

May the Lord bless you as you journey through this study!

A NOTE FROM THE AUTHOR

AM I KNOWN? AM I LOVED? AM I HOME?

Every human heart is searching for the answers to these questions. Yet when pain and heartache enter our lives, we feel betrayed and cry out one question: *God, do You see me?*

The answer is yes. He is Behind the Seen.

Because we live in a fallen world, each of us will inevitably face hard times, even painful ones. Who among us has never seen or felt the fallout of broken homes, broken lives, or broken dreams? Hagar is a great example of someone who discovered God during a difficult time. Maybe you have never heard of her. Or perhaps you came across her name in a study of the book of Genesis. But how much do you really know about this young slave girl? We often relegate her to the backstage as a minor character in God's redemptive story. *But was she?*

As I explored Hagar's story for another book I wanted to write, God continually amazed me as we journeyed together from the affluence of Egypt, into a life of slavery, to a desert of despair. It seemed the more I studied her life, the more I discovered about God. What began as a chapter evolved into a study all its own. Two years and several thousand hours of study and prayer later, the book you are holding came to be. Consider this your backstage pass to the life of Hagar.

I have never actually gone backstage during a live event, but I know that much more goes on behind the scenes than meets the eye. I invite you to come backstage with me and explore how God was involved in every detail of Hagar's life. Her story has all the ingredients of a Hollywood tragedy: betrayal, loss, abuse, crisis pregnancy, abandonment. . . . Does any of that sound painfully familiar?

Thankfully, Hagar's story does not end in despair. God was working Behind the Seen—just as He has in your life and mine—all along. As a matter of fact, Hagar emerges victorious! Hagar is an unsung hero if there ever was one.

Beloved, is the enemy using anything in your past to try to derail you from God's plan or to hold you back from experiencing God's joy to the fullest? Be assured that is not how your story will end. Just as God did for Hagar, when He enters your story, victory is already assured.

So strap on your sandals. We're heading into the desert. A place where we will encounter the "God Who Sees Me."

Your sister in Christ,

Shadia

> "The people who walked in darkness
> have seen a great light;
> those who dwelt in a land of deep darkness,
> on them has light shone."
>
> —Isaiah 9:2

INTRODUCTION

I DID NOT GROW UP GOING TO CHURCH OR READING THE Scriptures. As a matter of fact, I was thirty years old the first time I opened a Bible. Still, somewhere along the way, I picked up a few stories, all of which I dismissed as fairy tales and wishful thinking.

What about you? Regardless of how much or how little you know about Scripture, if I asked you to name a few famous Bible stories, I suspect you would be able to name at least one or two.

Perhaps you would think of Noah. After all, a worldwide flood makes for a remarkable story. Hollywood even made a few movies about it.

Or maybe Abraham would be first on your list. His mountaintop experience is required reading in every Sunday school class.

What about Moses? A slave turned prince runs away from his Egyptian palace into a barren desert, where God speaks to him from a burning bush. That's quite a story! But while Moses's miraculous encounter is exceedingly significant, he was not the first person to have a transformational experience with God in the desert. Actually, that honor went to a woman: a lowly, Egyptian, runaway slave named Hagar.

NOTES

PART I

WOUNDED

DISCOVERING GOD'S PRESENCE

LIFE IS FULL OF DETOURS.

This week, we will trace Hagar's origins through the story of Abraham and Sarah. As soon as the couple begins to make headway toward the Promised Land, they are diverted into Egypt, where trouble awaits. Could what appears to be a disastrous detour actually be a part of God's sovereign plan?

DAY ONE
Experiencing God's Presence in Life's Detours

When I was growing up, my family moved more often than I wish to count. By my thirteenth birthday, we had moved nearly a dozen times, from the hustle and bustle of New York City, to a quiet suburb outside tourist-laden Las Vegas, to Morocco, where donkeys, cars, and camels shared the roads. Next was a rent-controlled apartment in Queens, New York, where car horns and police sirens lulled me to sleep, followed by the eerie silence of a house atop a small mountain in upstate New York. Each place we lived had a culture all its own, and no matter where we went or how hard I tried, I never seemed to fit in. I either did not look right, act right, or talk right. Or all three!

Being repeatedly uprooted, trying to make new friends only to say good-bye a year later, and never feeling settled or having a place to call home was definitely challenging. Yet, looking back, I discovered those challenges created an advantage for me rather than a handicap. I am grateful for the lessons I gained in adjusting to change, which, as time went on, came a little easier. Because I lived a year in Morocco and have parents who each immigrated to the United States and speak several languages, I feel at ease around people who are different from me, even when I do not understand what they are saying.

PAUSE TO PONDER

How about you? Reflect on a time when you felt like you did not belong or fit in. Share one or two positive outcomes you gained from your experience.

Record your thoughts in the margin; do this for all Pause to Ponder sections.

Looking Back

Before we dive into the life of Hagar, let's spend some time exploring the backstory that led up to it.

We begin this week's lesson with one of the Bible's most renowned couples: Abraham and Sarah. Like many other stories from Scripture, it opens with God calling people out of their comfort zone. Ten generations and 367 years after the famous worldwide flood, a man named Abraham received a divine message from God. (Actually, his name was Abram at the time, and God later changed it to Abraham. God also changed Abraham's wife's name from Sarai to Sarah. To avoid confusion, I'm going to use Abraham and Sarah throughout this study, except in Scripture quotations that use the older versions of their names.)

Learn about Abraham's background by reading Joshua 24:1–3. What word best describes Abraham's father? Circle one.

shepherd   idolater   priest   elder   warrior

Does Abraham's upbringing surprise you? Why or why not?

Read Genesis 12:1–9. Which of the following statements best reflects Abraham's response to God's command?

He obeyed after receiving his wife's approval.

He waited for a more convenient time to travel.

He obeyed and went.

PAUSE TO PONDER

Think about a time when God asked you to step out in faith.

What was your initial response?
Were you hesitant? Expectant? Resistant?

Why do you suppose you responded the way you did?

Did God ask you to leave someone or something behind?

In what ways did the experience shape your relationship with God?

Genesis 12:1 really bothers me: "Now the LORD said to Abram, 'Go from your country and your kindred and your father's house to the land that I will show you.'" I do not know about you, but I like to know where I am going. For me, it is hard enough being directionally challenged without the added problem of not knowing where I am supposed to end up.

I get lost. *A lot.* My close friends know this and graciously cover me in prayer whenever I travel. The Bible teaches that God determines the time and place each of us is born (Acts 17:26). I wonder if He waited until the invention of GPS before sending me into the world.

I once remember driving with a new friend to a large park where we were planning to walk the trails. Within minutes of fastening our seat belts, I realized my friend was just as devoid of an internal compass as I was. This was a couple of years before smartphones, so neither of us had GPS on our cell phones. We could have printed out a map from the Internet, but because I had lived in the area for over twelve years, I did not think we needed one. I was wrong. For nearly forty-five minutes, we drove in circles, trying to find the park.

Exasperated, I called my friend Liz who was familiar with the area and my tendency to get lost. I could imagine her shaking her head as she recited the directions. When my friend and I arrived at the park, we realized it had been practically a stone's throw away the entire time we were driving. To this day, I still get lost and am often asked, "Why don't you use your phone's GPS?" To which I reply, "I do—once I realize I'm lost." Something about data and dollars and . . . sigh.

Walking by Faith

Abraham had no idea where he was going when God told him to leave. He had to trust God to lead him every step of the way. Talk about walking by faith!

Glance back at Genesis 12:4-8.

List each of the family members Abraham took with him.

What else did Abraham take with him when he set out for Canaan?

Read Genesis 11:30. What additional detail do we learn here?

Describe the location where Abraham called on the name of the Lord. Be specific.

Considering Abraham's family background, how much significance would you ascribe to Abraham's decision to call on the name of the LORD in Genesis 12:8? Place an X on the line to indicate your response.

not very significant _____ very significant

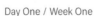 Explain your response.

In Joshua 24:3, Scripture teaches us that God Himself took "Abraham from beyond the River and led him through all the land of Canaan." Think back to the first time you sensed in your heart a longing for God. Do you believe God guided your steps to reach that point? Explain.

"The heart of man plans his way, but the LORD establishes his steps."

—Proverbs 16:9

In John 6:44, Jesus said, "No one can come to me unless the Father who sent me draws him." Take a few moments to meditate on that thought. Reflect on your own journey with God up to this point. Where would you place an X on the line?

I went looking for God _____ God came looking for me

Over the past week, how often did you call on the name of the Lord?

In my set daily prayer time

Whenever I needed something

Throughout the day

Only when I blew it

An Unexpected Detour

When God asked Abraham to leave nearly everything that was familiar to him, Abraham and Sarah packed up their little family and began the journey. However, just as they were starting to make some headway, the couple found themselves having to take a detour.

Read Genesis 12:10–16. Briefly summarize the events in your own words.

While Abraham was wise to take steps to protect his family from starvation, in fear for his life, he failed to protect his wife from the hungry eyes of Pharaoh. The servants of Pharaoh were so taken by Sarah's beauty (even at age sixty-five!) that when they told Pharaoh about her, he took Sarah into his home.

Read Genesis 12:17–20. What did God do and why?

What Pharaoh didn't know (in addition to Sarah being Abraham's wife) was that God's promise to Abraham, "I will make of you a great nation," was, by extension, also a promise to Sarah. And God's promise would not be thwarted.

Why do you suppose God stepped on to the scene in regard to Sarah, but He did not intervene to prevent the famine that drove her and Abraham into Egypt in the first place?

Coming Full Circle

Read Genesis 13:1–4; then answer the questions that follow.

Describe the place where Abraham built an altar and "called upon the name of the LORD" after departing Egypt.

Does this place sound familiar? (Hint: Glance back at page 22.) What conclusions can you draw?

Except for the sovereignty of God, the trip to Egypt would seem like nothing more than a temporary detour since, from there, Abraham journeys right back to where he started. Let's see if perhaps there is more to this story than taking an off-ramp to stop for dinner and load up on snacks.

....Your Turn ....

Sometime today or tomorrow, read Genesis 16 all the way through to gain an overview as we embark further on our journey with God Behind the Seen.

DAY TWO
Doubting God's Presence
When Your World Doesn't Make Sense

Years ago, while I was living in upstate New York, I had a cute, red Miata convertible with a removable hard top. One unseasonably warm spring day, I wanted to drive with the top down, but no one was at home to help me remove the heavy top. So I decided to do it myself. I unlatched the hinges and lifted the hard top a few inches. When my legs started shaking, I turned the top toward myself. I watched, helpless, as the metal corner screeched down the left rear panel of my car, tearing through the shiny red paint from top to bottom. I finally wrestled the top onto the driveway and then turned around to survey the damage. My heart sank as I gazed at the ugly, jagged scar on my beautiful little car.

PAUSE TO PONDER

Have you ever become impatient waiting for something or someone, perhaps even God, and decided to take matters into your own hands? What were the results?

The Offer

Read Genesis 15:1–6. What did Abraham long for?

Scripture clearly states, not once but twice, that Abraham was childless (verses 2 and 3). Take a few moments to meditate on Abraham's words: "Oh Lord GOD, what will you give me, for I continue childless. . . . You have given me no offspring."

Is there anything you long for (or have longed for) so much that, even if you were to be given everything else, it would not be enough? How can you relate to Abraham's heartache?

While we do not have the time to trace all the details of Abraham's life to this point, Scripture reveals that Abraham was quite favored. He had position, possessions, a beautiful wife, freedom, and God's personal blessing. But Abraham's heart ached for one thing above all else: a son. Yet God, who is all-powerful and who could give Abraham anything, chose first to offer Himself.

Write down what God said to Abraham, as recorded in Genesis 15:1.

Whenever God asks us to leave behind anything or anyone, resulting in a perceived loss, it is because He wants to satisfy our longings with something infinitely better: His presence.

Read Ruth 2:11–12. Compare "shield" in Genesis 15:1 and "wings" in Ruth 2:12. What (or whom) do each of these images point to?

 What other parallels can you discover between Ruth and Abraham?

PAUSE TO PONDER

> Why might God want us to desire a relationship
> with Him first, above all other desires of our hearts?
>
> Consider your deepest longing. What if, in the
> end, God chooses not to grant your request?
> Will you still be able to trust His plan for your life?

Refuse to Settle for Second-Best

God longs to give us the very best, which means God wants us to seek Him first. After God delivered Abraham's enemies into his hands (Gen. 14), He came to Abraham in a vision and said, "Fear not, Abram, I am your shield; your reward shall be very great." In the original Hebrew, the sentence structure of Genesis 15:1 creates a parallel between the words "reward" and "shield."[2] Whereas Abraham was looking for an earthly reward of a son (a worthy desire implanted by God Himself; see Gen. 1:28), God's promise here points to something exceedingly higher: the presence of God Himself (both in this life as our "shield" and into the next as our "reward"). When we seek Him first, not only will we experience the greatest relationship we could ever imagine, but He will also guard us against our own destructive tendency toward idolatry (placing something or someone, even one's own self, above God).

According to Abraham, who is at fault for Abraham being childless?

Abraham presumed that a servant, rather than a beloved son, would be his only heir. Then God told Abraham he would indeed have a son; more than that, he would have descendants too numerous to count. This is where God commends Abraham's faith: Abraham "believed the LORD" and God "counted" his faith as righteousness.

Describe several ways people try to earn God's favor by their own efforts.

Read Galatians 3:8. According to Galatians 3:8 and Genesis 15:6, what must precede righteousness (or justification)?

The word translated "justify" in Galatians 3:8 is *dikaio* in Greek. It is the same root word used throughout the New Testament for "righteousness" and can also be translated "declared [or made] righteous."[3]

PAUSE TO PONDER

How about you? Are you trying (or have you tried in the past) to earn God's favor—perhaps by investing more time in serving Him than in deepening your relationship with Him? If so, ask God to help you identify any false beliefs about Him that might be hidden in your heart. Record what God reveals to you.

Shifting Gears

As on any journey, sometimes we can coast through the valleys, and other times we need to climb some hills. In order to navigate the difficult terrain, we need to be prepared to temporarily shift gears. This is one of those times. We are about to tackle a small hill. Are you ready? Let's go.

List each group of possessions Abraham had accumulated while living in Egypt, in the order presented in the text. I listed the first one to get you started.

Sheep _____

_____

_____

_____

_____

_____

"And for her sake he dealt well with Abram; and he had sheep, oxen, male donkeys, male servants, female servants, female donkeys, and camels."
—Genesis 12:16

Take a few moments to examine this list. Record anything that strikes you as unusual.

Glance back to page 22 where you recorded everything Abraham took with him when he set out for Canaan. In addition to his family, what else did Abraham take with him?

Did you notice a difference in how the author describes what Abraham had with him in each case? In Genesis 12:5, the author simply writes that Abraham took "all their possessions . . . and the people they had acquired." However, the same author goes into far greater detail in Genesis 12:16 to list basically the same things. Nothing in Scripture is random. When something seems unusual, it is good to ask why. God's Word is like a treasure hunt. If we ask questions and do some research, we are bound to discover beautiful nuggets of insight.

In the Bible, the structure of the text can often provide tremendous insight into what the author wanted to emphasize. Did you notice in Genesis 12:16 that the only animals distinguished as male and female were the donkeys? I found that curious, so I did some digging. It turns out there are more than sixty references to the plural form of donkeys in the Bible. However, besides Genesis 12:16, there are only four instances where donkeys are distinguished as male and female. In each of the other four instances, the animals represent either an elaborate gift (Gen. 32:15 and 45:23) or God's blessing (Job 1:3 and 42:12), and the author always includes the exact number of animals, such as "twenty female donkeys and ten male donkeys."

When we take into account this scriptural pattern, along with Pharaoh's favor toward Abraham in Genesis 12:16, it seems likely that this list does, in fact, represent an elaborate gift given to Abraham by Egypt's wealthy ruler. However, in contrast to similar verses, in Genesis 12:16 this same author leaves out the number of animals. So why not simply say "donkeys," as he did with the sheep, oxen, and camels? Not only did the author separate the male and female donkeys, but he did not list them consecutively. Elsewhere in the Bible, the more valuable items, such as people, are often listed last (regardless of quantity), as in Genesis 32:5: "I have oxen, donkeys, flocks, male servants, and female servants." Given the curious arrangement in Genesis 12, it seems the author is drawing our attention to something about this list.

A literary pattern called chiastic structure is common in Scripture, whereby the author intersects mirror images of words, concepts, or events in order to draw the reader's attention to what the author wants to emphasize. To help readers see the pattern, biblical scholars typically use pairs of letters (such as A with A¹, B with B¹) to identify parallel words, phrases, or concepts when outlining a chiastic structure. Let's take a look at Genesis 12:16 by outlining the verse in this structure. (Note: I have added a general description after each item in the list in parentheses for further clarification.)

>   A   Sheep, oxen (animals, general)
>   >   B   Male donkeys (donkeys, gender specific)
>   >   >   C   Male servants (human servants, gender specific)
>   >   >   C¹   Female servants (human servants, gender specific)
>   >   B¹   Female donkeys (donkeys, gender specific)
>   A¹   Camels (animals, general)

Notice how the object (animals, general) in line A is similar to that in line A¹ (animals, general). The same is true for B and B¹ (donkeys, gender specific), and C and C¹ (human servants, gender specific). The author's goal is to draw our attention to the point where the parallels intersect.

Now, if the author had merely listed the people in the middle, it would be unusual, but not necessarily unique. However, he does more than that. The male and female slaves are sandwiched between male and female donkeys. Now that is a strange arrangement. As a matter of fact, nowhere else in the entire Bible does that arrangement appear. Why is that significant? Hang on. We're getting there.

> Read Genesis 16:1. What fact does the author repeat? (If you do not recall, glance back at Genesis 11:30.)

All of a sudden, Hagar appears on the scene. Where did she come from? The Bible offers no information about Hagar except for introducing her as an Egyptian slave girl belonging to Sarah, Abraham's wife. Because Genesis 12:5 tells us that Abraham had people and possessions in Haran, we can only wonder if Abraham and Sarah acquired Hagar while they were in Egypt. However, considering her ethnic origins, Abraham and Sarah's detour into Egypt, and all that we just gleaned from Genesis 12:16, I do not believe the author is leaving us to guess. You might be starting to wonder if *I* am taking *you* on a curious detour.

Recall from yesterday's lesson the events that led Abraham and Sarah into Egypt. When they left, taking hordes of animals and slaves with them, they traveled right back to where they started. Only then could Abraham resume his original course in response to God's call, "Go . . . to the land that I will show you" (Gen. 12:1).

Could it be that God was watching over Hagar and that He decided to remove her from Egypt and its pagan gods? Might He have orchestrated Abraham's side trip into Egypt, not because God needed to send Abraham and Sarah in, but because God desired to bring Hagar out?

This, my friend, is the wonderful sovereignty of God at work Behind the Seen.

....Your Turn ....

Think of a time you experienced a detour in your life. Looking back, are you able to see how God was working Behind the Seen in your situation? If so, complete the following sentence.

When I was _____ [approximate age(s)], I experienced a detour when _____ [describe the situation]. But God _____ [describe how God revealed Himself, or protected or comforted you, or used the events for good].

If you are unable to recognize God's presence in the situation, spend some time this week in prayer and ask God to help you see the ways He intervened or used the situation to accomplish something positive. Perhaps He has enabled you to have compassion for others in a similar situation. When you are ready, go back and complete the fill-in sentence as God enables you. (Note: There are a total of six fill-in questions of this kind throughout this study. These questions are important, as we will refer back to them when we near the end of our study.)

DAY THREE
Dismissing God's Presence as You Grasp for Control

Read Genesis 16:2-4. What was Sarah's complaint?

In ancient society, a man who remained childless was viewed as a tragedy. For a woman, barrenness was utterly shameful, leading people to suspect that God had cursed her.

> Contrast whom Sarah blames for her situation and whom she ultimately trusts to provide a solution.

> Contrast who previously declared a promise to Abraham in Genesis 15:4 and whose voice Abraham ultimately listens to.

What conclusions can you draw from these observations?

Misuse of Power

The text relates the events quite abruptly, which may be an indication of how quickly they unfolded. There is no evidence that Hagar was consulted or whether her feelings were ever considered. Sarah virtually issued a command to Abraham, which, in an ancient patriarchal society, was a bold move. And Abraham simply complied. No debate. No discussion. And for Hagar: no warning and no wedding. Why? Sarah's words offer us a clue: "I shall obtain children by her."

"Obtain children" is *banah* in Hebrew, which is one word. The word sounds like the Hebrew word for son (pronounced "ben"), but it literally means "to build." It is the same word used in Genesis 11:4, when the people of the earth all shared one language and came together, saying, "Come, *let us build ourselves* a city and a tower with its top in the heavens, and *let us make a name for ourselves*" (emphasis mine).

Oh, how many tragic stories are there of people trampling upon one another simply to "make a name" for themselves? Sadly, rather than trusting in God's plan, Sarah took matters, or rather her servant, into her own hands. Dragging Hagar in one hand and pulling the elderly Abraham in the other, Sarah set out to build herself a family.

It is worth noting that despite the practices of the surrounding cultures at the time, Abraham appears to have remained monogamous up to this point. Otherwise, he would have had no reason to lament before God, as we read in Genesis 15:2, that he was childless and presumed his servant would be his only heir.[4] The author

> "Then they said, 'Come, let us build ourselves a city and a tower with its top in the heavens, and let us make a name for ourselves.'" —Genesis 11:4

goes a step further to ensure the reader recognizes that, although Abraham would regrettably comply with Sarah's schemes, the idea both originated from and was orchestrated by Sarah, not Abraham. The language is reminiscent of Genesis 3.

For the following exercises, I recommend that you examine the Scriptures using the ESV Bible translation, or another more literal translation such as the NASB, NKJV, or KJV.

Read the second half of Genesis 3:6 and then complete the following sentence:

She _____ of its fruit and ate and she also _____ some to her _____.

Do the same thing for Genesis 16:3:

Sarai, Abram's wife, _____ Hagar the Egyptian, her servant, and _____ her to _____.

Now read Genesis 3:17 and fill in the following sentence:

And to Adam, [God] said,

"Because you have _____ to the _____ of your _____..."

Do the same thing for Genesis 16, the end of verse 2:

And Abram _____ to the _____ of _____.

Who would it seem Abraham was trying to please: God, himself, or his wife?

What other conclusions can you draw based on your observations of the text?

The Power of Words

Women can be so persuasive! Like any human trait, the ability to persuade can be used for good and God-honoring purposes, such as defending the weak or evangelizing the lost, or for bad and self-serving purposes. Just as Eve "*took the* fruit and *gave* it to *Adam* (her husband)," Sarah "*took* Hagar and *gave* her to *her husband*" (emphasis mine).

But wait. Each man had a choice to make with what he had been given. Regrettably, neither one made a good decision. Just as Adam "*listened* to the voice of [his] wife," Abram "*listened* to the voice of Sarai" (emphasis mine). The phrasing of these two verses—that the man *listened to the voice* of his wife—exists nowhere else in the Bible. It would appear, then, that the author is deliberately showing a parallel between the fall of mankind in Eden and Abraham's compliance with Sarah's schemes. Sadly, the apple did not fall far from the tree. I wonder if it ever hit the ground!

While Sarah blamed God for the problem, she did not seek Him for a solution. Instead, she came up with her own. And although Abraham experienced a direct revelation from God in Genesis 15:4—when "the word of the LORD came to him"—in Genesis 16:2, he instead "listened to the voice of Sarai." Whenever we follow a voice that is not in alignment with God's will, someone is bound to get hurt.

So many voices in such a brief passage! Yet there is one voice that remains absent: Hagar's. Being a slave left her with no voice and no choice. Even her body became an instrument of her mistress's problems and ambitions. No dream wedding or opportunity to build a better life for herself. Even her children would not be considered her own.

Still, while Hagar is certainly an innocent victim in this situation, let us not presume her to be altogether blameless. After all, Hagar, like the rest of us, suffered the effects of the Fall and sin's curse. If she had ever hoped to elevate her social status, giving birth to the patriarch's firstborn might very well do the trick. The fact that Hagar was quick to revel in her newfound condition speaks volumes for someone whose voice, up to this point, has remained entirely silent.

Warning: Danger Ahead

Rewrite the second part of Genesis 16:4 in your own words.

We do not know the exact details of Hagar's response, but the original Hebrew has the idea of Hagar "looking down" or having "looked dishonorably" on Sarah. Although Hagar may have justified herself in her own mind, in what ways was she disrespectful toward Sarah?

Do you believe Hagar was justified in her response? Why or why not?

List all the reasons Hagar may have had to despise Sarah when Hagar realized she was pregnant.

PAUSE TO PONDER

1 Peter 2:18 tells us, "Servants, be subject to your masters with all respect, not only to the good and gentle but also to the unjust." While this Scripture addresses the relationship between slave and master that was common in New Testament times, at the heart of Peter's teaching is an attitude of respect and servitude for those whom God has positioned in authority over us.

Is there an area of submission you struggle with? If so, bring it before the Lord right now. God is pleased when we bare our hearts to Him in humble confession. Share your thoughts.

SUPPLEMENTAL READING

DID HAGAR BECOME ABRAHAM'S WIFE?

The author continues to refer to Sarah as Hagar's mistress, reaffirming that Hagar's position had not changed. Theologian John Peter Lange explains that Hagar "is not so much the concubine of the husband [but rather a] *supplementary concubine of the wife*" (emphasis mine).[5] Sarah used Hagar to serve as her temporary surrogate in order to produce a child. Had Hagar been elevated to a higher position, such as that of a second wife, Sarah's statement in Genesis 16:2, "I shall obtain children by her," would be meaningless.

Old Testament scholar Gordon J. Wenham writes concerning Sarah, "The mistress could then feel that her maid's child was her own and exert some control over it in a way that she could not if her husband simply took a second wife."[6]

Confusion stems from the next verse, which states, "Sarai, Abram's wife, took Hagar the Egyptian, her servant, and gave her to Abram her husband as a wife." If this were the only mention of Hagar in Scripture, it would be reasonable to suppose the author is simply stating a fact. However, all other references to Hagar throughout the narrative—whether by Abraham, Sarah, the author, or God Himself—refer to Hagar as Sarah's servant. We need to examine why the word "wife" is used to refer to Hagar in verse 3, but nowhere else.

Like any other biblical interpretation, context is key. Throughout Genesis 16:1–3, every action and concept centers on Sarah, except when Abraham "listened to the voice of Sarah," which still circles back to Sarah. Sarah is on center stage here. By calling Hagar a "wife" in verse 3, the author is simply bringing to a close his presentation of the events from Sarah's point of view. To Sarah, Hagar was given to Abraham temporarily as a surrogate wife in order to produce a child *for her*. Once the deed was done, Hagar immediately reverted to her original status, which was never actually lost. For Hagar, at the end of the day (or night), a surrogate wife is not really a wife at all.

Just one chapter earlier, God commended Abraham for his faith. And while we know Abraham's faith was genuine, he allowed Sarah to persuade him in the wrong direction, reminding us that even godly men and women are prone to failure.

Slippery Slope

At a glance, the consequences of acting upon impatience seem far less serious than acting upon temptations stemming from things such as greed, lust, or envy. Yet it was precisely Sarah's frustration with God's schedule that prompted her decision to use Hagar to produce a child. Whenever we are tempted to question God's plan, wisdom, or goodness, we risk the sin of unbelief. And once we cross that line, sin has a way of quickly spiraling out of control.

PAUSE TO PONDER

Recall a time when you became frustrated
or angry about something that did not go your way.

Were you tempted to blame God? If so, how?

Did you seek to rally people around you?

In the end, did you take matters into
your own hands or do things God's way?

What were the results?

Empowered by Truth

Look up at least two of the following Scriptures relating to God's goodness. Rewrite the verse in the space provided as it appears in your Bible; then summarize what each verse says about God's goodness in your own words.

Reference	Write the verse	Summarize in your own words
Psalm 34:8		
Psalm 73:1		
Psalm 84:11		
Romans 8:28		

....................................Your Turn....................................

Meditate on these Scriptures. Is there a verse or concept that speaks to you personally, or one that you struggle with? Share your thoughts in the margin.

Sometimes we can be tempted to doubt God's goodness. Or we believe God is good, but we struggle to receive His goodness personally.

What are some practical ways you can counter the temptation to doubt God's goodness?

Write a prayer of gratitude to God for a specific way you have experienced His goodness this past week.

DAY FOUR
Fleeing God's Presence in the Midst of Mistreatment and Abuse

Read Genesis 16:5–6.

"If looks could kill." This is the expression that comes to mind when I read that Hagar "looked with contempt on her mistress." It seems her belly was not the only thing that started to swell. Perhaps a baby bump meant a bump in social standing as well, at least in Hagar's eyes.

These subtle cues may have gone undetected by Abraham. After all, he was in charge of leading hundreds, if not thousands (Gen. 14:14), of people through the desert, plus flocks and herds. Not only that, but in all likelihood, Hagar would have done her best to conceal her disdain from Abraham. The text offers no indication that Hagar occupied much of Abraham's concern. Whether he was aware of the brewing hostility between the two women or whether Sarah's outburst took him completely by surprise, Abraham considered Hagar to be Sarah's responsibility.

Retracing the Steps

When Sarah confronts Abraham, whom does she acknowledge as the one who placed Hagar in Abraham's embrace (or in his arms)?

How does Abraham describe Hagar?

What does Abraham tell Sarah to do?

The literal translation of Abraham's response, "Do as you please," actually has a positive tone. It is derived from the root Hebrew word *tob*, meaning "to be pleasing or good."

✎ List two or three ways Sarah could have handled the situation differently.

Interesting fact: Hagar is "a Semitic, not an Egyptian, name."[7] The name may arise from the rare Hebrew verb *hgr*, which has been translated by some biblical scholars as "to flee" or "flight," "fugitive," or "stranger."

How do you suppose Abraham's refusal to get involved in the conflict affected Hagar?

Standing on Sinking Sand

Because Abraham reaffirmed Hagar as being Sarah's servant, it seems evident that he did not view Hagar as his wife. He did not even consider her his concubine. This is apparent when we compare Sarah's complaint, "I gave my servant to your embrace," with Abraham's response. He actually uses a similar visual image: "Your servant is in your power," or literally, "Your servant is in your hand."

Poor Hagar. Taken into a man's chamber, but never into his heart; released by her mistress, but never set free. In one brief, heated exchange, Hagar was tossed back and forth as the couple tried to decide what to do with her. Finally, when Hagar realized her attempt to gain the upper hand had not worked, she ran away.

Describe the desperation of Hagar's situation. What are some of the reasons she may have wanted to leave?

As a single, unwed mother in an ancient society, what do you suppose were Hagar's chances of survival without God's intervention?

Compare the lives of single, unwed mothers in today's modern society with Hagar's. In what ways are they similar? How are they different?

PAUSE TO PONDER

What do you think? Are all people equally dependent on God for survival, whether single or married, living in poverty or affluence? Share your thoughts.

Read at least two of the following verses. What do the verses reveal about our dependence on God?

Psalm 24:1 Proverbs 16:9, 33 Isaiah 45:7 Acts 17:24-26

Behold Him Who Rides through the Deserts

Read the Scriptures printed in this section; then complete the following actions. Underline each group of persons God's heart beats for. Circle all of the ways God directly responds to their afflictions. Draw a box around every command God gives to His people.

"Sing to God, sing praises to his name; lift up a song to him who rides through the deserts; his name is the LORD; exult before him! Father of the fatherless and protector of widows is God in his holy habitation" (Ps. 68:4–5).

"Thus says the LORD of hosts, 'Render true judgments, show kindness and mercy to one another, do not oppress the widow, the fatherless, the sojourner, or the poor, and let none of you devise evil against another in your heart'" (Zech. 7:9–10).

"The LORD watches over the sojourners; he upholds the widow and the fatherless" (Ps. 146:9).

"O LORD, you hear the desire of the afflicted; you will strengthen their heart; you will incline your ear to do justice to the fatherless and the oppressed, so that man who is of the earth may strike terror no more" (Ps. 10:17–18).

"You shall not mistreat any widow or fatherless child. If you do mistreat them, and they cry out to me, I will surely hear their cry" (Exod. 22:22–23).

Look back over the verses and then complete the chart as follows: In the first column, list every word or phrase you underlined. In the second column, list each phrase you drew a circle around. In the third column, write the words or phrases you drew a box around. Next to each category of persons you entered in column one, write how many times each group appears in these verses. (I completed one to get you started.)

> "God is our refuge and strength, a very present help in trouble."
> —Psalm 46:1

God's heart beats for:	God promises to:	God asks us to:
Widows (4 times)	Watch over them	Show kindness to them

How do these verses contribute to your understanding of God's character?

In the Bible, there are more than fifty passages where God's protection, concern, and demand for justice for the sojourner (foreigner/stranger), the fatherless, and the widow are linked as one cohesive thought.

PAUSE TO PONDER

In what ways have you personally experienced God's intervention, either directly or through the actions of His people, at a time when you were vulnerable?

"For he makes his sun rise on the evil and on the good, and sends rain on the just and on the unjust."

—Matthew 5:45

The Illusion of Control

Because we live in a fallen world, all of us will experience some form of suffering. And just like Sarah and Hagar, we don't always respond admirably.

When Hagar was treated as chattel, she reacted with contempt. When Sarah was treated with contempt, she responded by bullying. When Hagar was bullied, she ran away. Just as in the Garden of Eden, all the enemy needs is one person to take the first bite to set in motion a tragic chain reaction.

For Hagar, running away likely offered her the temporary illusion of being in control. Even if she did not know where she was going, at least she could feel she was the one deciding which direction to take. In today's society, especially in the modern West, we are bombarded with messages designed to convince us that we can take care of our problems ourselves.

Jesuit priest Thomas Michel reminds us that Hagar's struggle is just as alive today as it was in ancient society, among "the low-born, hard-working domestic laborer, used and misused and cast out by her employers, the single mother abandoned by the father of her child, the foreigner and refugee far from her native land, desperately trying to survive, frantic in her maternal concern for the safety of her child—this Hagar I have met many times."[8]

Your Turn

Are there any areas in your life where you tend to dismiss God or struggle to recognize your dependence upon Him? Check all that apply:

☐ job / career   ☐ school / education   ☐ health   ☐ parenting

☐ marriage / relationships   ☐ freedom / safety   ☐ finances   ☐ home / possessions

☐ abilities / talents   ☐ air / water / food / clothing   ☐ ministry   ☐ other: _____

How can your perception of being able to take care of your problems yourself lessen your awareness of your complete dependence on God?

What are some practical ways you can counter these tendencies toward self-sufficiency, which is really pride?

Choose one or two specific action steps you will take this week, and write a prayer of commitment to God in the margin.

DAY FIVE
Marveling at God's Presence Behind the Seen

Read Genesis 16:7–8. Who meets Hagar and where does he find her?

> "Where shall I go from your Spirit? Or where shall I flee from your presence?"
> —Psalm 139:7

A Desert Encounter

This is the first time the Hebrew phrase *malak Yahweh*, "the Angel of the LORD" (meaning "Messenger of Yahweh"), is used in Scripture. This messenger declares to Hagar in Genesis 16:10, "I will surely multiply your offspring," which only God Himself could do. It seems, therefore, that this being is both God and God's messenger, perhaps alluding to the distinction among the Persons within the Trinity. Some scholars hold that the angel merely had the authority to speak the words of God, while others contend that this angel can be none other than the preincarnate Christ. One Bible scholar confesses, "The identity and function of the Angel of the Lord is also debated. In the Old Testament, the identity of the Angel can be difficult to distinguish from Yahweh Himself."[9] Let us pause to look briefly at one passage to see what we can discover.

Read Exodus 3:1–7, which describes Moses's encounter at a burning bush. List each way Scripture refers to God in verses 2 through 4. What conclusions can you draw?

In just two verses, God, the Lord, and the Angel of the Lord are presented as being one and the same. Whether this angel is the "preincarnate Christ" is hard to say; nevertheless, according to what we just read in Exodus 3, He is certainly God Himself. I love the fact that Hagar is the first person in the Bible to encounter the Angel of the Lord.[10] This concept can be challenging to grasp when Scripture teaches that no one can see God and live (Exod. 33:20 and John 1:18). In our fallen human condition, this is true: we cannot see God in all of His glory because it would literally annihilate us. When we are told that Hagar (or Abraham or Moses or others in the Bible) saw and spoke with God, or the Lord, or the Angel of the Lord, it is because God appeared in a form that enabled them to see Him. This does not mean they saw God fully revealed in all His glory.

Whether Hagar understood this we do not know; however, there is one woman who did. Although Hagar is the first woman to be visited by the Angel of the Lord, she is not the only one. This angel later appeared to Samson's mother, who was barren. When the angel visited her, he promised that she would conceive and bear a son. The angel then returned and spoke with both the woman and her husband. The husband was so alarmed that he told his wife, "We shall surely die, for we have seen God." But his wife responded, "If the LORD had meant to kill us, he would not have accepted a burnt offering and a grain offering at our hands, or shown us all these things, or now announced to us such things as these" (Judg. 13:2–3, 22–23).

This same God chose to speak with a lowly slave girl named Hagar. As a matter of fact, this angel is the first—and only—person in the narrative to speak directly to Hagar. The angel asked Hagar a two-part question.

Write the question along with Hagar's response.

How does Hagar describe where she came from? Circle one.

a town or city   a situation   a land or country   a person

Why do you suppose Hagar neglected to answer the second part of the question?

What might Hagar's response to the question "Where are you going?" reveal about her:

Emotional state

Plan of action

Understanding of her position in Abraham's household

Contrast Hagar's desert trek with Abraham's desert trek in Genesis 12.

Who was leading Abraham? Who was leading Hagar?

How was it going for Abraham? How was it going for Hagar?

What wisdom can you glean from these examples for your own life?

The Crossroads

Although Hagar failed to answer the second part of the question, and her response to the first part is somewhat elusive, we can certainly commend her for her honesty.

Perhaps having lived most, if not all, of her life as a slave, Hagar had never been asked a question that did not pertain to the needs or commands of others.

Up until now, we have not heard Hagar speak or be spoken to at all. Yet, when she says something for the first time, she is talking directly with God!

While God is always working Behind the Seen, here we get to see Him up close and personal. And who does He choose to speak with? A prophet? Not this time. A priest? Nope. He pays a visit to a lowly, pagan-born slave girl. Oh, I love how God's heart beats for women!

God Behind the Seen

In one sense, I can relate to Hagar. Many years ago, I also wanted to run away. For fourteen years, I had struggled in a codependent relationship with a volatile alcoholic. During the first year of our relationship, there were several incidents of physical abuse. After that, the abuse was primarily verbal assaults and threats. Because so many women (and men) suffer from ongoing physical abuse, I used to dismiss my suffering as "not so bad"; however, God has since revealed to me that the painful arrows of venomous words had actually left the deepest wounds on my heart. Dr. Carolyn Leaf, a highly respected cognitive neuroscientist and Christian author, teaches, "Words really do cause pain. Researchers have shown that hurt feelings from words affect the same area in the brain . . . as a broken bone or physical injury. So the old Scottish nursery rhyme of 'Sticks and stones will break my bones, but words will never harm me' is most certainly not true."[11]

Today, nearly nineteen years after my marriage ended, I can look back in amazement at all the ways God protected me. There were many times when I wanted to run away. I would drive my little red Miata for hours along winding rural roads, not knowing—or caring—where I was going. If the encroaching darkness of the night could not soothe the deep caverns of my heart, I would pull over to the side of the road and sleep.

Only now do I recognize the many ways God protected me, even though I did not know Him at the time. My car never broke down or ran out of gas. I was never harassed as I slept, despite my vulnerability in a tiny convertible in the middle of only-God-knew-where. I actually slept soundly, which gave me the strength I needed to face another day. Perhaps most amazingly, considering my already confessed poor navigation skills, I always found my way back. Truly, I now know that God was watching over me.

It breaks my heart that so many people suffer various kinds of abuse. I do not know what you might have endured, but of one thing I am certain: God knows, God saw, and God grieved. While He allows people the choice to use their power to hurt others, we must never confuse God's permission with His approval. God loves you, and He wants to redeem your story.

Pause to Ponder

Recall a time when you were mistreated or abused by another person; then answer the following questions (keep in mind that mistreatment includes mental or emotional abuse).

In what ways can you relate to Hagar?

Did you ever try to run away? Stuff your feelings? Avoid conflict? Or mask your pain with an addiction or other compulsive behavior? Explain.

If the abuse occurred at a tender age, how might those events have shaped how you respond to mistreatment as an adult?

Just as Hagar may have hoped Abraham would come to her defense, was there someone you hoped would stand by your side but did not?

...............................Your Turn...............................

Read Psalm 139:7. Recall a time when you felt mistreated or a time when you wished you could run away. Do you believe that God was watching over you in the midst of your situation? If so, complete the sentence below. (Remember, mistreatment may also include verbal, mental, or emotional abuse, such as mocking or bullying.)

When I was _____ [approximate age(s)], I felt mistreated or wanted to run away when _____

_____ [describe the situation]. But God _____

_____

_____ [describe how God revealed Himself, or protected or comforted you, or used the events for good].

If you are unable to recognize God's presence in the situation, spend some time this week in prayer and ask God to help you see the ways He intervened or used the situation to accomplish something positive. Perhaps He has enabled you to have compassion for others in a similar situation. When you are ready, go back and complete the fill-in sentence as God enables you.

Beloved, there is one Person who did come to your defense. Two thousand years ago. While the enemy planned to deceive you, control you, and destroy you, God sent His beloved Son to rescue you. We will explore this precious truth more fully in Week Six; until then, take courage: God wants to redeem your story.

Lesson Summary

What Scripture, statement, or thought was most significant to you this week? Write it below and then reword it into a prayer of response to God.

> "Blessed be the God and Father of our Lord Jesus Christ, the Father of mercies and God of all comfort, who comforts us in all our affliction, so that we may be able to comfort those who are in any affliction, with the comfort with which we ourselves are comforted by God."
>
> —2 Corinthians 1:3–4

A worship song that I enjoy, which powerfully captures the heart of this week's lesson, is called "Almighty God" by One Sonic Society. Perhaps you will enjoy it as well.

Notes

[1] Joni Eareckson Tada, *A Lifetime of Wisdom: Embracing the Way God Heals You* (Grand Rapids, MI: Zondervan, 2009), 94.

[2] Biblical Studies Press, Genesis 15:1 notes, *The NET Bible First Edition* (Richardson, TX: Biblical Studies Press, 2006).

[3] See *Young's Literal Translation,* the *Common English Bible,* the *Complete Jewish Bible,* or *Bible in Basic English.* Other variations of the word, such as "made right," or "put right," or "set right," are found in the *Good News Translation, The Message,* and the *New Century Version.*

[4] While some argue that Abraham may have previously tried to sire children with a concubine and failed, there is nothing in the text to support this view. Further, the author's mention of Abraham fathering more children later in life (Gen. 25) is positioned in the text only after the author records the death of Sarah.

[5] J. P. Lange, P. Schaff, T. Lewis, and A. Gosman, *A Commentary on the Holy Scriptures: Genesis* (Bellingham, WA: Logos Bible Software, 2008), 416.

[6] Gordon J. Wenham, *Word Biblical Commentary,* vol. 2, *Genesis 16–50* (Dallas: Word Books, 1994), 7.

[7] K. A. Kitchen, "Hagar," in *New Bible Dictionary*, 3rd ed., eds. I. H. Marshall et al. (Downers Grove, IL: InterVarsity Press, 1996), 439.

[8] Thomas Michel, "Hagar: Mother of Faith in the Compassionate God," *Islam and Christian-Muslim Relations* 16, no. 2 (2005): 99–104.

[9] J. A. McGuire-Moushon, "Angel, Critical Issues," in *The Lexham Bible Dictionary*, eds. J. D. Barry et al. (Bellingham, WA: Lexham Press, 2016), Logos edition.

[10] That is, after the Fall of Adam and Eve.

[11] Caroline Leaf, "Are the Toxic Words Spoken over and to You, Blocking Your Perfectly You?," *Dr. Leaf* (blog), May 17, 2015, http://drleaf.com/blog/are-the-toxic-words-spoken-over-and-to-you-blocking-your-perfectly-you.

NOTES

ENCOUNTERING GOD'S
PEACE

THIS WEEK, WE WILL EXPERIENCE THE DEPTHS OF GOD'S compassion through the eyes of Hagar, a runaway slave trying to outrun her circumstances along with her tears. Fleeing into the desert, she collapses in despair by a stream of water—completely unaware that she has landed precisely where God wants her.

DAY ONE
Looking for Love in All the Wrong Faces

Today we are going to temporarily put Hagar's story on hold while we read the story of another woman who experienced a divine encounter. However, rather than God finding her in a desert place, He found this woman in a deserted place.

Read John 4:1–30.

This passage is the longest recorded conversation between Jesus and another person in the Bible. The woman is simply identified as "a Samaritan woman," meaning she was a mix of both Jewish and Gentile descent, a "half-breed," despised in the minds of pious Jews at that time. During Jesus's day, Jews looked with contempt upon Samaritans, which the writer points out in verse 9, in case the reader

49

was unaware. As a matter of fact, no self-respecting rabbi would dare set foot in that region, choosing rather to take a much longer route in a deliberate attempt to avoid the area. Yet the author of the Gospel of John writes that Jesus "*had* to pass through Samaria" (John 4:4; emphasis mine).

When Jesus arrived, He sat down by a well to rest. It was noon—the hottest part of the day. Typically, women waited until the cool of the evening to head out to the nearest well. Bustling with activity, the well was the heartbeat of community life. The entire village depended on it for the life-giving water it supplied to their families and livestock. Every evening, the women would congregate there, sharing stories of their children and families, catching up on the latest news, and drawing water to take back to their homes.

But this Samaritan woman ventured out to the well at the most uncomfortable time of day, when the area would most likely be deserted.

Living Water

Several aspects that appear in the stories of both Hagar and the Samaritan woman are listed in this section. Take a few moments to refresh your memory by glancing back at Genesis 16. Then, in the space provided, record any similarities you can discover in the lives of these two women. I completed the first one to get you started.

Nationality/identity

> Both women lacked a secure national identity. Also, Hagar's son would be of half-Jewish and half-Gentile descent, just like the Samaritan woman.

Position/standing within her community

Marital status/relationships

Water

Reread John 4:13-15 and then answer the questions that follow.

What two promises does Jesus make to the Samaritan woman for all those who drink the water He offers?

What two reasons does the woman give for wanting the water Jesus offers?

List any observations you can make.

Right Place, Right Time

While the Samaritan woman is clearly attracted to the idea of never being thirsty again and freedom from the daily chore of drawing water, she mentions something else, too. Notice the clarifier she adds to her comment about drawing water: "Sir, give me this water, so that I will not be thirsty or *have to come here* to draw water" (John 4:15; emphasis mine). The woman would avoid the place altogether if she could. Curiously, the author used similar wording to describe Jesus's mind-set in verse 4, which is difficult to discern in the English translation. However, rather than the emphasis being negative (wanting to *avoid* a place), the phrase in verse 4 has a positive connotation whereby Jesus was *compelled to go* ("had to pass") through Samaria. The place the woman dreaded coming to the most was the very place Jesus was determined to enter.

Both Hagar and the Samaritan woman went to get water—one in a desert place and the other in a deserted place. And it was precisely in those moments when God showed up. But before either woman could recognize who was speaking to her, she first needed to recognize the deeper thirst hidden in her heart.

The Real Dilemma

Glance back once more at John 4:14-16. Contrast Jesus's promises in verse 14 with his instruction to the woman in verse 16. What observations can you make? How might these be related?

By coming to the well at the most uncomfortable part of the day, the woman could avoid having to face anyone. She confessed her wish to not have to come "here" to draw water—a place that for other women bubbled with life and community but which for her had likely become a deep, friendless void. As if that were not enough, Jesus then tells her, "Go, call your husband." It was just another jab into the dark caverns of her heart. Yet what was true for her is also true for each of us: as painful as our woundedness is, God often uses our deepest hurts to open our hearts to His presence.

But Jesus is not finished; He has one last thing to say to her . . . "and come here." *Come to the very place you wish you would never have to return to.* But something in the text has changed. Previously, when the author wrote that Jesus "had to pass [or go] through Samaria" and that the woman did not want to "have to come" to the well any longer, the Greek form of the verb in both cases is more passive, meaning it is describing something that is happening to the person. The word also has the idea of movement (coming, going, crossing, or passing through). However, when Jesus says to the woman "come here," it is a command to take action—a decision she must make. Further, this word does not include the idea of something ongoing; rather, the emphasis is on having *arrived.* She has a choice to make: she can continue going her own way, ever wandering but never arriving, or she can accept Jesus's offer: *come to me . . . and you will finally arrive.*

PAUSE TO PONDER

Reread John 4:16–17.

How did the woman respond to Jesus's command?

Knowing full well that the woman did not have a husband, what motivation may have been behind Jesus's command?

The Announcement

Read John 3:22–29. How does John the Baptist refer to Jesus?

In all four Gospels, this is the first—and only—direct reference to Jesus as bridegroom.[1] The common definition of bridegroom is simply a man who has just married or is about to be married. Because this is the only reference of its kind, where it is placed in Scripture is important.

Where does the author position the only illustration of Jesus as bridegroom relative to the story of the Samaritan woman?

Do you find the position of this illustration in the text significant? Encouraging? Inconsequential? Share your thoughts.

PAUSE TO PONDER

Scripture teaches that Jesus will one day come for His people, the church, as a bridegroom comes to bring home his bride (John 14:2–3 and Rev. 19:6–8).

Close your eyes and try to imagine what that might be like. What images come into your mind? What feelings stir within your heart?

If you find this imagery difficult, confess your struggle and ask God to help you see what might be hindering you. Write a prayer in response to what God reveals to you.

The Debate

Jesus broke with tradition and took the road less traveled to meet and talk with the Samaritan woman. After sending His disciples on an errand, He waited alone at the well, providing the perfect opportunity to speak with the woman privately and intimately. At first, she seemed uncomfortable with Jesus prying into her personal relationships. Who can blame her? As Jesus recounted her past, she tried to deflect the conversation by engaging Him in a debate about religion and the places people should go to worship.

Not once but twice, she reminded Jesus of her religious heritage, "our father Jacob" (verse 12) and "our fathers" (meaning Abraham and Jacob, verse 20), revealing her beliefs of how and where a person should worship. Jesus turned her notions about worship upside down by revealing it is not about ancestors or mountains or heritage, but a relationship: *God the Father came looking for her.*

Reread John 4:21–23. How many times does Jesus refer to God as Father? Do you find this to be significant? Why or why not?

Up until this encounter, the handful of verses in the New Testament where God is spoken of as Father[2] have all been in relation to Jesus as Son. This is the first time[3] in the New Testament that God is revealed as being a Father not only to Jesus but to all "true worshipers," those who "worship in spirit and truth" (verse 23). And who does Jesus choose to be the first recipient of this good news? A prophet? Not this time. A priest? Nope. He chooses to share the good news first with an outcast, "half-breed," adulterous woman. Amazing!

Drawing Near

Try to imagine what it would have been like to be that Samaritan woman. Her past hurts have been dredged up and her immorality exposed, but she is waiting for the Messiah. Then a man sitting at a well asks for a drink. No fancy parables, no poetic speech, and no flashes of lightning. Her hope for deliverance—her greatest need—has arrived, and He is calmly sitting right in front of her, face-to-face.

Seeing past her history and her hurts, Jesus peered directly into her broken heart. Time and again she had pursued love and affection, hoping to find someone who would truly cherish her forever. Perhaps she was used or abandoned after being enticed by empty words and empty promises from those who could never mend her broken heart.

To have had five husbands is rare even in our day, but in Jesus's time it was outright unthinkable. While men were permitted to seek a divorce (Deut. 24:1), if a divorced woman were to remarry, society scorned her as adulterous, deserving or not. Whether divorced or widowed, whether tender relationships or difficult ones, each separation would have left a deep wound. Then along comes Jesus, gentle and humble, pursuing her, wooing her. Here is a man who knows the depths of her hurts and the longings of her heart, but rather than being deterred or overwhelmed, He draws closer.

What do you suppose may have been the Samaritan woman's greatest need?

A Broken Past

While we do not know the details of this woman's background, there is no shortage of psychological studies linking a woman's history of multiple and/or unhealthy relationships with an absent father (whether he is absent physically or emotionally). We hear the tragic stories all too often: a painful childhood produces an adult plagued with insecurities who repeats the cycle of destructive relationships, further wounding, rather than mending, her broken heart.

I know her story all too well. My parents divorced when I was twelve. Not long afterward, I began looking for love in all the wrong faces. I was fourteen when I carelessly gave myself to a nineteen-year-old man. I believed he loved me (as best as a fourteen-year-old understands love), only to discover he was dating several other girls at the same time. A few months after we broke up, I met someone closer to my age. Less than a year later, I became pregnant by him and, feeling like I had no other choice, had an abortion. He moved away shortly after that. By the time I was seventeen, I had engaged in a string of brief relationships, trading sex for the short-lived illusion of being loved. Like bait being attacked on a hook, each encounter left me more wounded and broken than the last. When I finally met a man who was willing to stay, I never stopped to examine what I had caught. The abuse started as soon as we moved in together. In the beginning, there were incidents of physical abuse. In time, it transitioned to mostly emotional and mental abuse. He always said he was sorry and I always believed him.

It's a simple yet tragic truth: wounded people attract wounded people. My idea of love was that the one who stayed with me must be the one who really loved me. Perhaps the Samaritan woman thought the same way. I can only imagine how deeply this must grieve our Lord, who created women to be cherished, protected, and treated with tenderness and dignity. Instead, all too often, many of us relinquish pieces of our hearts again and again, desperately looking for love in all the wrong faces.

Then along comes Jesus, gentle and humble, pursuing us, wooing us. A man who knows the depths of our hurts and the longings of our hearts, but rather than being deterred or overwhelmed, He draws closer.

A New Beginning

The last segment of the story is truly inspiring.

Reread John 4:28–30.

How does the woman describe Jesus to the people?

How does her description compare with her description of the coming Messiah in verse 25?

Where does she lead the people?

Compare this place with her words in verse 15. What observations can you make?

"Come!" Can you imagine? The very location that just a short time ago served as a painful reminder of her broken heart and empty soul has become a place overflowing with living water. Where she once dreaded to draw water, she now draws people. Those who once shunned her, perhaps even used her, have become the first to whom she unashamedly introduces her Savior! Only now do we see why Jesus *had* to pass through Samaria.

"See!" Her eyes have been opened. The word for see (*idete* in Greek) does not mean something that is simply visualized, but rather something that has been personally experienced. For years, she had been looking for love in all the wrong faces. Suddenly, the Lover of her soul opens her eyes to see the One who loves her more than life itself. She has seen the Messiah, she has tasted the living water, and her life is forever changed.

Oh, I can hardly wait until we get back to Hagar's story so you can see the beautiful red bow that ties these last pieces of the stories together.

···Your Turn ···

Have you ever traded away something or compromised your beliefs in an effort to feel loved by a person? If so, what were the results?

Do you believe that God's love is sufficient to fulfill the deepest desires of your heart? Have you placed your trust in anyone or anything to fulfill the longings that only God can fill? Explain your response.

Beloved, there is only One who can give us true, unconditional, perfect, eternal love. You can stop searching for Him. He came looking for you. When Jesus finds a receptive heart longing for true love, He is compelled to enter.

A worship song that I enjoy, which truly captures the heart of today's lesson, is called "Glance" by Misty Edwards.

DAY TWO
Thirsting for God's Peace in the Desert of Abandonment

Reread Genesis 16:7-8. Briefly summarize the events in your own words.

We pick up Hagar's story with her running away along a desert road toward Shur, a wilderness spanning hundreds of miles in the Sinai Peninsula. This road is believed to be a common caravan route of that day between Palestine (Canaan) and Egypt. Perhaps Hagar thought she could run all the way back to Egypt.

Identity Crisis

It is not difficult to sympathize with Hagar's identity crisis. She was likely acquired by Sarah at a young age.[4] By now, her homeland is a distant memory, along with its pagan gods. She has no real relationship with the father of her child, and her mistress would probably love for Hagar to simply disappear. With no real home of her own, it is no surprise that Hagar does not know how to fully answer the question "Where have you come from and where are you going?"

"The greatest crime in the desert is to find water and keep silent."

—Ancient Arab proverb

Encountering God's Peace

PAUSE TO PONDER

> In what ways are the questions "Where have you come from?" and "Where are you going?" connected to one another in your own life?

God Sees

How does the angel address Hagar in Genesis 16:8? Do you think this is significant? Why or why not?

Rather than focusing on her past or her future, when the Angel of the Lord finds Hagar by a spring of water, He wastes no time reaffirming her current position as the "servant of Sarai." Apparently, even conceiving a child for the patriarch of God's future covenant nation did not change Hagar's status.

Her one and only encounter with a man leaves her pregnant, rejected, unloved, and unwanted. No bridegroom, no wedding, and no husband. No one to speak tenderly to her, to cherish her, or to protect her. She is left with none of the things a woman's heart longs for. Oh, how my heart aches for Hagar!

But what does she experience instead? A face-to-face encounter with the Angel of the Lord! God actually came looking for her. The verb translated "found" in verse 7 is not passive but active. In the same way that Jesus actively sought out the place where the Samaritan woman would come to draw water, the Angel of the Lord came purposely to meet Hagar by a spring of water.

SUPPLEMENTAL READING

GOD WILL WIPE AWAY EVERY TEAR

I was surprised to learn that the word translated "spring" in Hebrew is *ayin*, which is also translated "eye." I was curious as to why two seemingly different things were called by the exact same word, so I did some research. I discovered that the word *spring* relates to *eye* because of tears. The prophet Jeremiah lamented, "My eyes are a fountain of tears" (Jer. 9:1), and the author of Lamentations wrote, "My eyes flow with rivers of tears" (Lam. 3:48).

During a recent prayer time, God revealed to me a wound of rejection that I had kept buried for over eighteen years. Although I had long forgotten about it, God had not. And He wanted to heal me of anything that stood in the way of my trusting Him fully. After He showed me my hurt, He gave me time to grieve. I cried out to Him my sorrow, releasing into His hands the deepest, darkest corners of my heart.

Then I opened my Bible to Revelation 19:11, where I gazed upon the words that reminded me Jesus is "Faithful and True." The moment I saw those words, tears began to fall uncontrollably. At one point, I lifted the open Bible to my eyes, as if I could somehow unite my tears with His Word . . . as if I could somehow touch my Lord by touching His Word. When I lowered my Bible in front of me, it was no longer open to Revelation 19. I do not know how I got there, but my Bible was now open to Revelation 7. Did the pages move when I was not looking? Did the ceiling fan cause them to turn? It does not really matter. All I know is that my tears had landed on these words: "For the Lamb in the midst of the throne will be their shepherd, and he will guide them to springs of living water, and God will wipe away every tear from their eyes" (Rev. 7:17). I sat amazed as I pondered once again the awesome truth that I serve the Living God.

For several minutes, I gazed at the tear-soaked page. Overcome by His love, I took a picture so that I would never forget the tender love of my Father and Lord, who met me right where I needed Him most. Even now, the page still carries the memory of that day. The droplets of tears changed my Bible forever. The page is no longer smooth, but indented where the tears had fallen. All around the indents are distinct ripples, as if pointing to the place where God's Word absorbed my tears. What an intimate God! Whenever I open my Bible to that page, I can't help but praise Him as I am reminded anew of His amazing love.

Theologian Charles Spurgeon beautifully captured God's tender compassion when he wrote, "A Jesus who never wept could never wipe away my tears."[5]

PAUSE TO PONDER

Read the quote in the margin. Do you agree with this statement? Why or why not?

"A Jesus who never wept could never wipe away my tears." —Charles Spurgeon

The Offer

"If anyone thirsts, let him come to me and drink" (John 7:37). At the place where Hagar saw a spring, God saw her tears. In the silence of a deserted well, Jesus heard the cries of a Samaritan woman's broken heart. Our God is bigger than our wounds and His love is greater than our sorrow. In Jesus Christ, there is no thirst too great that He cannot quench it.

Just as Hagar is the first woman[6] in the Old Testament to have a direct encounter with God, the Samaritan woman is the first woman in the New Testament to whom Jesus directly reveals His identity.[7] Truly, God's heart beats for women, for the hurting, the lost, and the outcast. And I, for one, am so thankful!

Just as He promised the Samaritan woman, Jesus promises to all who come to Him, "Whoever drinks of the water that I will give him will never be thirsty again. The water that I will give him will become in him a spring of water welling up to eternal life" (John 4:14).

I will never forget the day I took God up on His offer. It was June 1998. I had only been going to church a few months and did not know a single Bible verse. With my face buried in the living room carpet, I prayed to God, daring to believe He could hear me. I told God that if He was real, I wanted Him to hear my prayer, which sounded something like this:

> God, if You can hear me, please forgive me for living my life my way. I'm sorry for all of the mistakes I've made. Thank You, Jesus, for dying on the Cross for my sins. Please come into my life and make me the person You want me to be.

The next morning, I woke with a peace unlike anything I had ever known, which remains with me to this very day.

To all who take to Jesus their hurts, heartaches, burdens, and regrets, He offers a second chance. Romans 10:9 promises, "If you confess with your mouth that Jesus is Lord and believe in your heart that God raised Him from the dead, you will be saved."

······································Your Turn ·····································

Let the words of Jesus sink deep into your heart. "If anyone thirsts, let him come to me and drink. Whoever believes in me, as the Scripture has said, 'Out of his heart will flow rivers of living water'" (John 7:37–38).

How would you describe your greatest need right now?

Have you received Jesus Christ as your Lord and Savior?

If you have previously received the gift that Jesus offers, how have you experienced Jesus's promise that "out of [her] heart will flow rivers of living water"?

If you are unsure or undecided, consider the impassioned words of the apostle Paul, who wrote, "I tell you that the 'right time' is now, and the 'day of salvation' is now" (2 Cor. 6:2 NCV). In the margin, write a prayer expressing where you are and what might be holding you back. Be honest with God. He loves you and deeply desires a relationship with you.

If you have decided to accept God's gracious gift—the forgiveness of your sins through the death and resurrection of His Son Jesus Christ—and you choose from this day forth to follow Jesus as your Lord, record your prayer in the margin. Include today's date, and ask God to lead you to a healthy, growing church home. Then share your news with a friend, your group leader, or another member of the study. They'll be thrilled!

DAY THREE
Embraced by God When No One Knows Your Name

Let's do a quick review. Hagar was a slave, under the authority and protection of Sarah, and by extension, Abraham. When Sarah decided her own problems required intervention, she used Hagar to get what she wanted, then mistreated her when things did not go her way. If that were not bad enough, Abraham refused to get involved in the ensuing conflict, and in turn, Hagar ran away. Used, abused, and from Hagar's perspective, twice betrayed. A tragic chain of events that too many of us can identify with.

There is not enough room to write all of the heartbreaking stories that could be told. Yet the question I have heard at the end of many such stories is the same: "Where was God?" While I believe it was part of God's plan to bring Hagar out of Egypt and introduce her to Himself, God never orchestrates or condones sin.

PAUSE TO PONDER

Reflect on a time when you felt betrayed or misled. (You may even have felt betrayed by God Himself.) If you could go back and speak to yourself at that time, what would you say?

Next, complete the following sentence:

When I was _____ [approximate age(s)], I felt betrayed or misled when _____ [describe the situation]. But God _____ _____ [describe how God revealed Himself, or protected or comforted you, or used the events for good].

If you are unable to recognize God's presence in the situation, spend some time this week in prayer and ask God to help you see the ways He intervened or used the situation for good. Perhaps He used the events to draw you closer to Himself. When you're ready, go back and complete the fill-in sentence as God enables you.

The Good, the Bad, and the Ugly

One of the reasons God's Word is so deeply treasured by His people is that it makes no attempt to hide the truth: the good, the bad, and yes, the ugly. Even God-fearing people like Abraham and Sarah can be tempted to give in to irresponsibility, jealousy, and cruelty. Aren't you grateful that this is not sugarcoated in Scripture? I sure am.

> Before we dive into today's text, please reread Genesis 16:1–6. Carefully examine the dialogue between Abraham and Sarah. How do they refer to Hagar, and how many times do they refer to her by name?

Running Away

> Read Genesis 16:7–14. (Verses 7 and 8 are review.)

I imagine that Hagar had never felt so alone. Perhaps she ran away thinking, *No one will miss me.* Or, *If I run away, then they'll miss me.*

When the Angel of the Lord meets Hagar in the desert, He addresses her by name. As a matter of fact, He is the only person in the entire narrative to call her by name.

How might hearing the Angel of the Lord speak her name have influenced Hagar's choice of referring to God as "the God Who Sees Me" in verse 13?

Contrast what Hagar's life might have been like as a single, pregnant, homeless woman in the desert with her life as Sarah's servant. How does this comparison shed light on the angel's command in Genesis 16:9 to return home and "submit to your mistress"?

A Difficult Road

The Scripture is not clear as to exactly how Sarah treated Hagar. The phrase "dealt harshly" can also be translated "afflicted" or "humbled." It is the same root word that the Angel of the Lord used in Genesis 16:9 when he commanded Hagar, "Return to your mistress and *submit* to her" (emphasis mine). The use of parallel wording reveals that God fully understood what Hagar had endured; nevertheless, He made no promise to change the situation. Though Hagar had been disrespectful toward Sarah, God took notice when Hagar was treated unjustly.

Describe all the ways Hagar and her unborn son would be provided for if she returned to Abraham and Sarah.

God Watches Over You

Although Scripture does not mention whether God or Abraham or anyone else confronted the elderly Sarah about her behavior, there is nothing in Scripture to presume God condoned it in any way. As a matter of fact, though the Old Testament had not yet been written, it would provide specific regulations regarding the treatment of servants (or slaves). For example, they were to be granted a weekly Sabbath rest along with everyone else (Exod. 20:10; Deut. 5:14) and invited to celebrate with the entire community the various feasts and festivals throughout the year (Deut. 16:11, 14).

God does not change. Justice and kindness are His heart's desire, and He is especially concerned for those who are most vulnerable.

64

Read Matthew 23:12 in the margin. Think about a time
when God asked you to humble yourself and do something
difficult that you now understand He was doing with your
best interest in mind; then answer the questions that follow.

How did you respond?

What were the results?

If you could go back in time, is there
anything you would do differently? If so, why?

"Whoever exalts himself
will be humbled, and
whoever humbles himself
will be exalted."

—Matthew 23:12

Just as the Angel of the Lord did not promise to change Hagar's circumstances, the New Testament encourages perseverance for slaves who suffer harsh treatment. In Ephesians 6:9, the apostle Paul warns, "Masters, do the same [i.e., do the will of God from the heart][8] to them, and stop your threatening, knowing that he who is both their Master and yours is in heaven, and that there is no partiality with him."

Read Philippians 2:3-11; then answer the following questions.

What form does the Scripture say Jesus took, according to verse 7? Circle one.

king   human/man   servant/slave   priest

Why did God exalt Jesus? Because Jesus _____.

was compassionate   is God's Son   loved people   humbled Himself

How did Jesus humble Himself?

How are humility and obedience linked in this passage?

For many of us, we can be obedient without being humble—appearing moral or religious on the outside without surrendering our hearts and will to Jesus as Lord. However, it is impossible to be truly humble before God without also a sincere desire to serve Him in complete obedience. When Jesus "humbled himself by becoming obedient," the condition that led to His exaltation was not His outward obedience, but His inward humility. There is only one active verb in this sentence, which is "humbled". Becoming obedient is an adjective in the original Greek. In other words, obedience is what humility *looks like*. For the Son of God, Creator of life and heaven and earth, becoming obedient to the point of death—even death on a cross—is the ultimate act of humility.

PAUSE TO PONDER

Is there an area or situation in your life where you find it difficult to be humble? If so, take a few moments to meditate on Philippians 2:3–8. Then list one or two practical steps you will take this week to follow Jesus's example of humble obedience.

The Big Picture

So often we want God to address the faults and failures of those around us. Yet the only person each of us has any control over is our self. Notice that the only mention of Sarah manifesting harsh treatment—whatever it was and however inappropriate it was—occurred after Hagar began to "despise her mistress."[9] Let's try to put this further into perspective.

Glance back at Genesis 12:2–4; then answer the questions that follow.

How old was Abraham when God promised to bless him and make his name great?

According to Genesis 16:2–3, how long had Abraham and Sarah been in Canaan when Sarah decided to use Hagar to build a family for herself?

Genesis 17:17 reveals that Abraham was ten years older than Sarah. What age then was Sarah when she gave Hagar to Abraham?

Assuming Sarah was married in her early childbearing years, approximately how long had she been living with the heartache of being unable to conceive a child?

10 years   20 years   30 years   40 years   50+ years

Finally, how quickly did Hagar's behavior take a turn for the worse?

Now, try to imagine yourself in Sarah's sandals. Putting aside for a moment how Hagar arrived in her condition, how might the haughty attitude of a young, pregnant slave have affected you at this point?

While we cannot excuse Sarah's unkind treatment of Hagar, sometimes it is helpful to try to see a situation from the other person's point of view. There is no evidence of a pattern of abuse. Scripture never indicates there was further mistreatment. Considering the fact that Hagar's pregnancy was Sarah's own idea, and that Hagar's unborn child was Abraham's own flesh and blood, it is possible that Hagar's flight into the wilderness may have distressed Abraham and Sarah both.

"Faith sees the invisible, believes the unbeliev-able, and receives the impossible."

—Corrie ten Boom, Holocaust survivor

PAUSE TO PONDER

Have you ever waited on God for the fulfillment of a godly desire? Are you still waiting? If so, how long did you wait (or have you waited)? In what ways can you sympathize with Sarah?

The Promise

God does not often call us to an easy road, but His ways can always be trusted. Despite how Hagar may have felt, Scripture assures us that she was never alone. God not only saw and heard Hagar in her affliction, but He comforted her with a promise.

What did God promise to Hagar, according to Genesis 16:10? Circle one.

freedom from slavery   a husband   a multitude of offspring   riches

In what ways does this promise parallel God's promise to Abraham in Genesis 15:5?

How might this news have encouraged Hagar?

Hagar is the only woman in Scripture to whom God directly promised a multitude of offspring. Whereas Sarah will certainly be blessed with similar and more far-reaching promises, as we will soon discover, God bestows upon Hagar His personal blessing of "a multitude" that cannot be counted.

························· Your Turn ·······························

Reflect on God's kindness in the life of a pagan slave girl. Does it surprise you? Encourage you? Explain.

Examine each area in the following chart and ask God to reveal any ways you might be striving to "make a name for yourself." Check all that apply.

☐ job / career	☐ school / education	☐ health
☐ marriage / relationships	☐ freedom / safety	☐ finances
☐ abilities / talents	☐ air / water / food / clothing	☐ ministry
☐ parenting	☐ home / possessions	☐ other: _____

Does this list look familiar? Glance back at Week One, the end of Day Four, and record any similarities you discover.

How can striving to make a name for yourself hinder your ability to experience God's peace in your life?

What practical steps will you take this week to counter the temptation to "make a name for yourself"?

Write a prayer of commitment to God in the margin.

Although the people of Babel tried to establish a name for themselves,[10] Sarah tried to build a name for herself, and Hagar tried to claim a name for herself, in the end, only God's Name is worthy of praise.

DAY FOUR
Clinging to God in a Hostile World

While we want to stay centered on Hagar, we do not want to gloss over the difficult pronouncement God makes in Genesis 16:11–12 concerning her unborn son. Just as the promise God made to Abraham in Genesis 12:3 hints at future hostility, God reveals that the future of Hagar's son holds hostility as well.

A Divine Pronouncement

> Reread Genesis 16:11–12. In what ways does this hostility mirror Hagar's current situation?

In Hebrew, "wild donkey" is actually one word (*pera*). It is a noun; there is no adjective. It simply refers to donkeys that roam free.

The illustration of a "wild donkey" or "wild ass of a man," whether pertaining to the child or to his descendants, is debated among scholars.[11] One writes, "Ishmael and his descendants will be wayward and headstrong. Ishmael and his kin will also be aggressive and combative, prone to conflict."[12] Another suggests, "The prophecy is not an insult. The wild donkey lived a solitary existence in the desert away from society. Ishmael would be free-roaming, strong, and like a bedouin; he would enjoy the freedom his mother sought."[13]

The phrase "he shall dwell over against all his kinsmen" (as translated by the ESV) has also been translated "he will live to the east of all his brothers" (NASB) or "he shall dwell in the presence of all his brethren" (NKJV). All of these are considered more literal translations; as such, there is no consensus concerning the interpretation of this verse. At times, Scripture will allude to both a literal meaning (present and physical) as well as a symbolic meaning (future and spiritual). Perhaps more than one meaning is intended for this text as well.

Take a moment to examine Job 39:5–8, which is printed below. Notice its poetic structure and similarities to the divine pronouncement of Ishmael's birth.

> Who has let the wild donkey go free?
> Who has loosed the bonds of the swift donkey,
>   to whom I have given the arid plain for his home
> and the salt land for his dwelling place?
>   He scorns the tumult of the city;
> he hears not the shouts of the driver.
>   He ranges the mountains as his pasture,
> and he searches after every green thing.

Some view the prophecy concerning Ishmael in the larger context of God describing his prodigy as enjoying a free, unrestrained nomadic existence. Others interpret the description as relating to Ishmael personally—either positively, as being independent and free, or negatively, as being undisciplined and hostile.[14] While the meaning of Genesis 16:11–12 is debated, there are several things we can glean from this Scripture.

The first thing we notice is its poetic structure. One purpose of using this method in Scripture is to heighten the emotional charge of the words for the reader. If God simply wanted to make a statement, such as, "Your son will have an independent spirit," or "He will not get along with his brothers," He could easily have done that. Instead, God inspired the author to use the more complex and dramatic literary form of poetry in order to draw special attention to the text. The second thing we notice is that God names Hagar's child. In this detail alone, we find that Ishmael belongs to quite a select group.

Named by God

Below is a list of every person in the Bible whom God personally and directly named before he was born.[15] See if you can match each one with the general meaning of his name. Bible references have been included in case you need them. I completed two to help get you started, as the meanings of these two names are not obvious in the text. (Hint: The name Solomon is related to the common Hebrew greeting spoken today, *Shalom*.)

Ishmael (Gen. 16:11, 17:20)	He laughs
Isaac (Gen. 17:17, 19)	God heals
John the Baptist (Luke 1:13–14)	The Lord saves
Josiah (1 Kings 13:1–2; 2 Chron. 34:1–8)	Peaceful
Solomon (1 Chron. 22:9)	God hears
Jesus (Matt. 1:21)	God is gracious

What general observations can you discover about this list?

What observations can you discover about Ishmael in particular? (Hint: Ponder the biblical citations for each name in chronological order.)

Not only is this list quite short, but also, without exception, every name reflects a positive attribute of God Himself, including laughter! Furthermore, you may have noticed that not only is Ishmael included in this list, but he is also the *first* person named by God before his birth.

As we move through Hagar's story, we will see that God's concern for Hagar extends to her son Ishmael as well. Write the meaning of Ishmael's name below.

How tender that God would give Hagar's son the name Ishmael. For Hagar, her own son would become a permanent reminder that God heard her cries and was intimately concerned for her in her affliction.

PAUSE TO PONDER

Examine the meaning of each name in the previous list. Describe one or two ways you have personally experienced one or more of these aspects of God's character in your own life.

A Heart in Need of the Healer

When I reflect back on my life, I can see that some of the darkest seasons were followed by some of the richest experiences of God's love, comfort, and peace. When I hear a song, read a poem, or see a painting that I find particularly stirring, I will sometimes research the artist to learn what inspired him or her to create it. Often the most heartrending creations are those that pour forth from the depths of a wounded soul. These songs, poems, or pictures resonate with us because very often they were birthed during a personal crisis, or a "dark night of the soul."[16]

Our hearts echo their pain. And the pain reminds us that the saying "Time heals all wounds" is simply not true. More often than not, it buries them deeper, but the truth is that beneath every person's layers of battle scars, heartbreaks, and broken dreams lies a heart in need of a healer.

PAUSE TO PONDER

Pastor and author Chuck Swindoll writes, "Tucked away in a quiet corner of every life are wounds and scars. If they were not there, we would need no Physician. Nor would we need one another."[17] Do you agree? Why or why not?

In what ways have you personally experienced God's healing in your own life?

Trusting His Plan

Our finite minds and wounded hearts may struggle to grasp why God sometimes waits to reveal Himself until after we go through a dark season. Yet if He is truly good, all-wise, and infinitely loving—and He is all of these—we can trust that He has a purpose, even if we do not yet understand His plan.

Take a few minutes to meditate on the Scriptures that follow. Underline each attitude or response the author expects of us. Then place a box around each of God's promises.

"Trust in the LORD with all your heart, and do not lean on your own understanding. In all your ways acknowledge him, and he will make straight your paths" (Prov. 3:5–6).

"The LORD is a stronghold for the oppressed, a stronghold in times of trouble. And those who know your name put their trust in you, for you, O LORD, have not forsaken those who seek you" (Ps. 9:9–10).

"Humble yourselves, therefore, under the mighty hand of God so that at the proper time he may exalt you, casting all your anxieties on him, because he cares for you" (1 Pet. 5:6–7).

"You keep him in perfect peace whose mind is stayed on you, because he trusts in you" (Isa. 26:3).

"Father to the fatherless, defender of widows—this is God, whose dwelling is holy. God places the lonely in families" (Ps. 68:5–6 NLT).

Based on the preceding exercise, complete the chart that follows. In the column entitled "Our Part," list each word or phrase you underlined. In the column entitled "God's Promise," list each phrase you drew a box around. I completed the first one for you.

Verse	Our Part	God's Promise
Proverbs 3:5–6	*Trust God with all of my heart.* *Do not lean on my own understanding.* *Acknowledge Him in everything I do.*	*God will make my paths straight.*
Psalm 9:9–10		
1 Peter 5:6–7		
Isaiah 26:3		
Psalm 68:5–6		

......................................Your Turn......................................

Review the table you just completed by reflecting on God's promises in the last column. Which promise best describes your greatest need right now?

Using your own words, rewrite the verse(s) into a prayer of faith.

DAY FIVE
Resting in God's Peace for Your Future

The first year or so after I became a Christian was quite difficult. Even though my husband and I had both made a profession of faith, had been baptized, and were regularly attending church, we still had a very unhealthy relationship. He struggled with alcoholism and fits of rage, and I suffered from codependency and depression. It was a tragic and toxic mix not unlike the experiences of many others.

Less than a year after I gave my life to Jesus, my husband left and filed for divorce. That was almost twenty years ago. While God has mercifully healed me of the debilitating nightmares that plagued me for some time afterward, there is one particular night during the last year of my marriage that is forever seared into my memory. It was the night God spoke to me.

My husband had been drinking and was itching for a fight. I bolted upstairs to our bedroom, locked the door, curled up into a ball, and rocked back and forth on the bed. As I had done countless times before, I shut my eyes as tight as I could, trying to escape into that dark cavern of my mind where everything ceased to exist, including me. It was my hiding place and after so many years of retreating there, it had become very familiar. Only this time, before I could get there, I sensed God speaking to me. His voice was as close to audible as I could imagine. He told me to call a friend from church.

At the time, I did not know my friend very well, but God's presence and gentle persistence leaned into me until I picked up the phone by the bed and dialed her number. I do not remember what I said to her, but I will never forget the soothing words that poured through the phone into my bleeding heart. She opened her Bible and slowly read Psalm 91.

Being a newborn Christian, I did not cry out or pray—I didn't even know *how* to call on God. Yet God heard my cry . . . and answered me. To this day, Psalm 91 remains one of my most treasured psalms. God's precious Word comforts me with His promise that He is my refuge. These are the words I cling to whenever I feel overwhelmed or frightened. Genesis 16:11 tells us that God heard Hagar's misery, even though Scripture presents no evidence that Hagar audibly cried out to God.

> "Misery sighs; the sighs ascend to God; hence misery itself . . . is a voiceless prayer to God."[18]
> —Commentary author's remarks regarding Hagar in Genesis 16

PAUSE TO PONDER

Do you believe God hears your misery? Why or why not?

God Is Our Refuge

Reflect on Psalm 34:4–7. Then, following my example in the chart, record every action taken by the psalmist, each action of God, and each outcome. (Note: Not all columns will have the same number of fill-ins).

Psalmist	The Lord (or Angel of the Lord)	Outcome
Sought the Lord	*God answered*	*Delivered from all my fears*

When you encounter trying circumstances, to whom do you instinctively turn first for help? Why?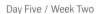

Think of a time when God intervened on your behalf in a difficult situation. In what ways can you identify with the psalmist?

Take some time to meditate on Psalm 34:4–7 or, if you prefer, Psalm 91. In the margin, record anything you sense God is saying to you.

The God Who Sees Me

Reread Genesis 16:13–14. Read verse 13 twice, and at least once out loud.

Try to imagine for a moment that you are Hagar. If someone were to ask you if you would trade anything—even a chance to erase all you had endured to this point—for a personal encounter with the Living God, would you do it? Why or why not?

How can Hagar's description of God as a god "who sees me" offer comfort to you when you find yourself frightened and alone?

Don't you just love Hagar's courage? She does not wait for God to introduce Himself. She does not even ask His name. Rather, Scripture says she tells Him. "She gave this name to the LORD who spoke to her: 'You are the God who sees me'" (Gen. 16:13 NIV). That takes guts! I do not know about you, but I might think twice before being so bold as to ascribe God a name. After all, I could get zapped! But if I let my head get in the way of my heart, in a split second my chance would be gone.

Not Hagar. She seized the opportunity. And I believe God smiled.

Eyes to See

Let's jump ahead briefly to the New Testament and look at another pivotal verbal exchange. Read Matthew 16:13–17.

Who does Jesus say gave Peter the ability to recognize Jesus's divinity?

Who do you suppose gave Hagar the ability to recognize the One who spoke with her in the wilderness?

Peter was raised in a traditional Jewish family, so he would have been very familiar with the Torah (the Hebrew Bible). He had also been a follower of Jesus for over a year when this exchange took place.

Contrast Peter's traditional Jewish upbringing against Hagar's pagan background. Was either one in a better position to recognize who was speaking without divine intervention? Does this encourage you? Why or why not?

Just as God did for Peter, He opened the eyes of Hagar's heart. "You are the God who sees me!" She did not need to wait for her head to catch up before announcing what God had enabled her heart to grasp. Imagine what our churches today would be like if they were filled with more people like Hagar!

Encountering God's Peace

A Well of Remembrance

One minute we see an oppressed runaway slave who could easily have fallen into a bottomless pit of self-pity, bitterness, anger, or despair. The next minute, we see a bold and courageous servant of God. No one can encounter the Living God and remain unchanged.

Hagar stands alone in the entire Bible as one who ascribes a name to God. Her divine encounter was so remarkable that a well was later named in remembrance of the events. In addition, her story is recorded in God's Word as an everlasting testimony of God's presence in the lives of people, even runaway slaves.

Comfort in the Chaos

Read Genesis 16:15–16.

Even before the child was conceived, Sarah claimed the child for herself. Not only that, but Abraham and Sarah both would have viewed Hagar's unborn son as rightfully belonging to them. Keep these thoughts in mind as you answer the next question.

 Glance back at Genesis 16:11. Why do you think God chose to announce Ishmael's name not to Abraham or Sarah, but to Hagar?

While God would send Hagar and Ishmael back to live under the protection and godly influence of an imperfect couple, imagine Hagar's delight in knowing that God Himself assumed the task of naming her child.

Although Hagar's words are not quoted in the text, by the time she returns to camp, we have no doubt that she has spoken to someone of her divine encounter. She had a choice . . . and now she has a voice. And as a result, "Abram called the name of his son, whom Hagar bore, Ishmael" (Gen. 16:15).

Let's Review

Whose idea was it for Hagar to conceive a child?

Who laid claim to him as her own before the child was born?

Who does the author state bore a son to Abraham, according to Genesis 16:15?

How many times does the author repeat this fact in Genesis 16:15–16?

In ancient languages like Hebrew, there are no punctuation marks, upper- versus lowercase letters, or different fonts to add emphasis to a text. Repeating a phrase once would add some emphasis. Stating it a third time is the author's way of saying, "You don't want to miss this!"

As the author ushers Sarah into the background (beginning at Genesis 16:7 and continuing until Genesis 17:14), the story of Hagar takes center stage. Sarah's sudden absence from this scene might be compared to Hagar's utter silence throughout the previous scene. Based on Abraham naming his son Ishmael, we can presume Hagar must have related the events she experienced in the wilderness to either Abraham or Sarah (or perhaps others as well). Then the author goes out of his way to record that "Hagar bore" three times, each time linking back to Abraham. That takes a lot of effort when we realize the original text was carved with a chisel into stone![19]

Why do you suppose the author went to such lengths to emphasize the fact that Hagar birthed the child to Abraham?

Courage in the Camp

Up until now, Hagar was effectively unseen and unheard, presented as simply an Egyptian slave, separated from her family of origin, with no husband and no children. But she was never unseen by *El Roi*, the "God Who Sees Me." He chose a desert of despair as the place where He would reveal Himself to her and assure her that she had a hope and a future.

In the midst of the wilderness and her woundedness, Hagar discovered she was known and she was loved. Her encounter with God gave her the courage to obey His voice and return to Abraham and Sarah, but she did not return the

same. She had a voice. And she had a place. While she would remain the servant of Sarah, Hagar would also be known as the mother of Ishmael, Abraham's son, whom God Himself named "God hears."

························· Your Turn ·······························

What about Hagar's story up to this point do you find most encouraging?

What can you learn from Hagar's example of obedience?

Father, our hearts go out to Hagar, who suffered so much, and yet, in Your mercy, You revealed Yourself to her as El Roi, the "God Who Sees Me." You pursued her in the midst of a desert of despair—where she was forever changed. Thank You for opening our eyes to Hagar's story. Truly, nothing happens without Your knowledge. You had a purpose for Hagar's life just as You have a plan for each of us. Give us courage, O Lord, to walk the path You have carved out for each of us. Grant us humble hearts to follow Hagar's example of trust and obedience. We pray this prayer in Jesus's precious and holy name. Amen.

Lesson Summary

What Scripture, statement, or thought was most significant to you this week? Write it down and then reword it into a prayer of response to God.

The tender worship song "Does Your Heart Break" by *The Brilliance* beautifully captures the heart of this week's lesson.

Notes

[1] Indirect references in the Gospels include Jesus relaying the parable of the ten virgins in Matthew 25 and Jesus responding to a question on fasting in three of the four Gospels.

[2] Prior incidents in which God is presented as Father in the New Testament include:

- Jesus as a boy in the temple, saying he was in "my Father's house."
- Jesus's baptism, when God said, "This is my Son."
- John the Baptist testifying that Jesus is the "Son of God."
- Nathanael confessing in John 1:49, "You are the Son of God!"
- Jesus overturning the tables of moneychangers at the temple, which he calls "my Father's house" in John 2:16.
- Jesus teaching that God "gave his only Son" in John 3:16.
- John the Baptist being the first, after Jesus, to call God Father, but in the context of the Son, saying, "The Father loves the Son" in John 3:35.

[3] "First time" in this context refers to chronological events. Jesus does speak of God as Father in Matthew 5 in his Sermon on the Mount; however, chronologically, this encounter with the Samaritan woman occurs first.

[4] Scripture teaches that Abraham and Sarah lived in Canaan for ten years after returning there from Egypt. If Hagar had been among the slaves given to Abraham and Sarah during their stay in Egypt, as many scholars deem probable, and Hagar is now of childbearing age yet still unmarried, though it was common for slaves to marry, it is likely that Hagar was a pre-teen or teenage girl when she entered Sarah's service.

[5] Charles H. Spurgeon, "Jesus Wept," *Metropolitan Tabernacle Pulpit* 35, no. 2091 (1889), http://www.spurgeongems.org/vols34-36/chs2091.pdf.

[6] That is, after the Fall of Adam and Eve.

[7] The Samaritan woman was the first, but not the only, woman in the New Testament to whom Jesus directly revealed his identity. See John 11:25–27.

[8] See Ephesians 6:6.

[9] Of course, this is not to say that giving Hagar to Abraham in the first place in order to produce a child was not also inappropriate, even if it was a common practice among the surrounding cultures at the time.

[10] See Genesis 11:4.

[11] S. A. Magallanes, "Ishmael, Son of Abraham," in *The Lexham Bible Dictionary*, ed. J. D. Barry et al. (Bellingham, WA: Lexham Press, 2014), Logos edition.

[12] J. D. Barry et al., Genesis 16:12, *Faithlife Study Bible* (Bellingham, WA: Logos Bible Software, 2012).

[13] Biblical Studies Press, Genesis 16:12 notes, *The NET Bible* (Richardson, TX: Biblical Studies Press, 2006).

[14] Magallanes, "Ishmael, Son of Abraham."

[15] Other references include Isaiah 49:1, which points to the coming Messiah, and Jeremiah 1:5, which states God knew the prophet before he was born; however, there is no indication that God named him. Isaiah 8:3 records God giving a name to the prophet's son; however, most biblical scholars consider the name symbolic.

[16] The term *dark night of the soul* was originally coined from the title of a literary masterpiece authored by Saint John of the Cross, who was a sixteenth-century monk. This poem, along with additional writings, was later published in a book with the same title.

[17] Charles R. Swindoll, *Day by Day with Charles Swindoll* (Nashville: Thomas Nelson, 2000), 233.

[18] J. P. Lange, P. Schaff, T. Lewis, and A. Gosman, *A Commentary on the Holy Scriptures: Genesis* (Bellingham, WA: Logos Bible Software, 2008), 417.

[19] Or clay tablets.

PART II

WANDERING

NOTES

RESTING ON
GOD'S
PROMISE

THIRTEEN YEARS HAVE PASSED WHEN HAGAR LEARNS that Sarah would soon give birth to a son. Insecurity and fears quickly resurface, yet in the midst of Hagar's heartache, God institutes a special covenant with Abraham. Would Ishmael be included?

This week, we will discover how to rest in God's promises when our world seems to be falling apart.

DAY ONE
Humbled by God's Great Promises

Not long ago, I was invited to speak at a church located approximately ninety miles from my home. Given my poor navigation skills, I printed and reviewed the directions the night before. The route seemed relatively straightforward—even for me. I was nearly beside myself when I arrived that Sunday morning without ever getting lost along the way. However, as I was driving home, I somehow missed my exit. And that was not the worst part: I kept going!

I knew I had passed my exit, but like a deer in headlights, I stared straight ahead, frozen in my seat, unable to think. *You did it again*, I scolded myself. *You missed your exit*. Being mentally and emotionally drained from sharing my testimony and speaking on a very sensitive topic (abortion), my mind went blank as I kept on driving . . . and driving . . . and driving. Because I needed to keep my eyes on the road, I couldn't fumble with my iPhone's GPS. *You should have learned how to use Siri*, I reprimanded myself. *What's the point of having a voice command feature on your phone if you are not going to use it?* I kept on driving.

Making a U-turn

Perhaps I thought that if I stayed on the road long enough, the exit would come back around. Seriously, I do not know what happens to me when I get lost, but it is never good. Eventually, I had the sense to take an off-ramp and turn around.

Sometimes, the only way to get back on the right track is to make a U-turn. A full 180 degrees—no more and no less. Twenty minutes and half a dozen exits later, I was finally home. A few days later, I figured out how to use Siri. Lesson learned.

Sometimes, the only way to get back on the right track is to make a U-turn.

PAUSE TO PONDER

We all get lost from time to time.
Sometimes we lose our way spiritually, too.

Describe a time when you continued going your own way even though it was in the wrong direction. Looking back, what "lesson learned" did you gain from the experience?

Everything Seems to Be Going Along Just Fine, When . . .

In this week's lesson, we find Abraham at center stage. Before we dive into the details, let's get an overview of the chapter. Sit back, relax, and open your Bible to Genesis 17.

Please read all of Genesis 17. How many times does God describe His covenant or promises as "everlasting" in Genesis 17:1–21?

Over thirteen years had passed since Hagar's divine encounter in the desert. All that time, Abraham (and perhaps Sarah as well) had been raising his son Ishmael, who was growing into a young man. Scripture gives no indication that Abraham, or anyone else in the narrative, had received any further revelations from God. Then one day, God stopped Abraham in his tracks. God reveals to Abraham that his son Ishmael was not the child God had promised him (Gen. 15:4). All of a sudden, Abraham and Sarah discover that the direction they had been heading all this time was, in fact, the wrong direction.

How does the Lord introduce Himself in Genesis 17:1?

What comes to mind when you think of the word *almighty*?

Look up *almighty* in a Bible dictionary or standard dictionary. Rewrite the definition using your own words.

What was Abraham's immediate response when the Lord appeared and spoke to him?

The Bible is filled with examples of external behaviors that can have an effect on us spiritually, such as singing praises to God (present in nearly one-third of the psalms, as well as many other books in the Old Testament), or combining fasting with prayer (Neh. 1:4; Dan. 9:3; Luke 2:37; Acts 13:2–3 and 14:23). Praying in the prostrate position (with face down to the ground) is another example (Ezra 9:5; 2 Sam. 12:16; Matt. 26:39). Prior to a few years ago, I rarely did this. But I have since found that this is a wonderful way to humble my heart before God, who is altogether holy.

PAUSE TO PONDER

Think of someone you know who has a strong walk with God.

What do you suppose contributes to him or her having a strong walk with God?

If you are not sure, consider contacting the person to ask what has helped foster his or her relationship with God. Come back and share what you learned.

"The LORD appeared to Abram and said to him, 'I am God Almighty; walk before me, and be blameless....' Then Abram fell on his face."

—Genesis 17:1-3

Looking Back

From Genesis 12 through Genesis 15, Scripture portrays various responses of Abraham regarding his interactions with the Lord. Match each one in the table to its corresponding verse.

Scripture Reference	Abraham's Response
Genesis 12:4	Questioned the Lord
Genesis 12:7 (also 13:18)	Believed the Lord
Genesis 13:4	Called on the name of the Lord
Genesis 14:22	Obeyed the voice of the Lord
Genesis 15:1–2	Built an altar to the Lord
Genesis 15:6	Swore an oath to the Lord

How would you describe Abraham's relationship with God up to this point, based on these passages?

SOMETIMES, GOD ORDERS ICE CREAM

Having a relationship with God is a tremendous joy and privilege, yet sometimes we make it too complicated. I had been at my desk all day, struggling to write today's lesson and getting nowhere fast. At one point, I thought I heard God say in my spirit, "Let's go for a walk." However, because I was not sure, I dismissed it. Besides, it was hot outside. So I stayed at my desk, papers and notes and my Bible spread out everywhere, trying to suppress the nervous energy which was now causing my legs to bounce. Then I heard it again: "Let's go for a walk."

When the Spirit nudges you once and you are not sure, God is gracious—the second time, it is best to take notice. I put on my sneakers, and just as I was leaving, I remembered that I needed something from the convenience store located a few blocks away. Thinking I might stroll by the store on the way back, I grabbed a few dollars from my wallet, stuffed them into my pocket, and walked out the door. I headed toward the park as I usually do, talking with God along the way (not out loud of course, in case I scare the neighbors). Then I saw it: an ice cream truck had stopped by the playground.

As luck would have it (though I suspect it was more than that), I had money in my pocket. A smile crept across my face. *When was the last time I bought an ice cream from a truck?* I wondered to myself. Almost immediately, my mood brightened. I waited my turn in line, feeling like a giant kid among the children giggling all around me.

As God and I continued walking and talking, I savored each bite of my orange creamsicle, marveling at how easily my frustration and discouragement began melting away. It was then that God spoke to my spirit, "You see; it does not have to be so complicated." And I knew exactly what He meant. I had been wrestling with a lot of heavy theology, and in doing so, I was losing focus on the heart of today's lesson. Only later did I realize the added irony that today's text begins with God's simple invitation, "Walk with me."

Read Genesis 12:1–7 and Genesis 17:1–4. Compare and contrast what God says in each encounter and Abraham's response. In what ways does it seem their relationship changed over time?

"Walk with Me"

The verb *walk* in Genesis 17:1 is in a grammatical form called the imperative, which simply means it is being spoken as a command or request. God's statement "walk before me" has the idea of "accompany me" or "come/go with me." When I think of God's invitation to Abraham, I am reminded of Jesus calling his first disciples, as recorded in all four Gospels: "Follow me!"[1] And while the words of God to Abraham as well as Jesus's words to his first disciples are a command, the call is personal. The Creator of the universe is inviting mortal men into fellowship with Himself.

I remember the first time I clearly sensed God asking me to follow Him. Only a few months after I had prayed and asked Jesus to be my Lord and Savior, divorce papers arrived. Shortly thereafter, I was praying one morning when God asked me to entrust my husband into His hands. You see, I had spent most of my adult life trying to be my husband's savior, and it was time for me to let go of my misguided, even dysfunctional, sense of responsibility. At one point, I envisioned myself walking with the Lord and looking behind me at my husband and asking God, "What about him?" God answered, "He is my concern. You, however, must follow me."

PAUSE TO PONDER

Describe a time when you experienced a personal invitation or call from God. Perhaps He asked you to trust Him in some area. Or leave something or someone behind and follow Him. How did you respond? What were the results?

"Be Blameless"

Read the following passages. Who is being described? What does it look like to be blameless according to these verses?

Genesis 6:8-9

Job 1:1

Luke 1:5-6

Being blameless before God is not something any of us can do; rather, it describes what we ought to be.

In Hebrew, the word blameless is *tamin* and has the idea of completion or perfection. It is not something any of us can do; rather, it describes what we ought to be. In effect, God is saying to Abraham (and everyone else who belongs to God), imitate (walk with) me, and in so doing, be perfect. Sounds like a tall order to me; however, God does not see us as we see ourselves. He sees Behind the Seen—He sees who we are becoming through Him.

Read the following passages. What additional information does Scripture reveal concerning those the Bible describes as blameless?

Genesis 9:20-21 (see also Gen. 7:6 for perspective)

Job 3:1; 40:1-2, 6-8

Luke 1:13, 18-20 (see also Luke 1:7 for perspective)

 What conclusions can you draw?

To be blameless or righteous in God's eyes can seem like a tall order; however, God knows our weaknesses. To "walk with God" arises from faithful devotion and a sincere desire to obey God—not sinless perfection.

Our Citizenship Is in Heaven

One commentary author writes, "The idea of walking before God is language used in Mesopotamian texts to denote one's allegiance to a king. It is a figure of loyalty to royalty."[2] As citizens of a country governed by the people rather than ruled by a king, this concept can seem foreign to those of us who live in the Western world. Rather than individual loyalty to a king, our allegiance is better understood as a shared national pride or patriotism. However, as Christians, we are all citizens of the kingdom of heaven (Phil. 3:20). Not only do we have a king, but He is God Almighty, to whom is owed our complete adoration, allegiance, and worship.

"But our citizenship is in heaven . . ."

—Philippians 3:20a

.......................Your Turn.......................

When you pray, how often, on average, do you physically come before God Almighty "on your face"?

daily   weekly   rarely   I have never done this

When you do position yourself before God in this humble posture, in what ways, if any, does it impact your time with God?

If you rarely or have never done this, why not try incorporating this into your prayer or worship time this week? Come back and record in what ways, if any, it had an impact on your time with God.

DAY TWO
Surrendering to God's Wise Path

Several years ago, I was facing a crossroads in my career and ministry, and I made an appointment with my pastor to seek his advice. I had a lot on my plate. God was opening doors for ministry; at the same time, I was doing contract work to pay the bills. I also volunteered at my church and served on the Board of Directors for our local pregnancy center. In the midst of all this, a great job opportunity arose, but it would require a substantial time commitment, leaving me little time to do anything else. I did not know what to do, but knew I could not do it all.

At the Crossroads

The morning of my appointment arrived. Sitting in my pastor's office, I explained my situation; then I waited. After praying silently, he looked up and simply asked, "Have you considered enrolling in seminary?"

Come again, pastor?

He continued, "Seminary. As I was praying, that's what God brought to my mind."

Well, it crossed my mind once a few years ago as a fleeting thought . . . maybe some day . . .

We prayed together and I thanked him. My heart was stirred within me. *Seminary? Could God really be calling me to go to seminary?* Western Seminary had a campus just twenty minutes' driving distance from my apartment. After a few days, I called their office. When I learned it was too late to apply for the upcoming term, a swell of emotions took me completely by surprise. I quickly ended the call as I tried to control the tears pouring from my eyes. *I have to wait?* I did not even know I wanted to go to seminary that badly. It felt as if God had planted a desire in my heart that, before then, I had not even known was there.

Over the next two months, I collected my academic records, gathered letters of recommendation, and submitted my application. Again . . . I waited. When the envelope arrived in the mail a few months later with the school's bright red logo in the corner, I could hardly contain my excitement. Before I opened the envelope, questions flooded my mind. *Will I soon be going to seminary? What does God have in store for me? What is my life going to be like?* Standing in the middle of the driveway, I opened the envelope and began reading.

Dear Shadia, I am pleased to inform you . . .

Seminary! This is going to change everything! Still today, I laugh and shake my head, thinking, *I went to see my pastor in order to get something off my plate, and instead more was piled on.* Each of us has ideas of what our future holds. If someone had told me years ago that I would one day graduate from seminary and write Bible studies, I would not have believed it, but God has blessed me with the privilege to do precisely that. None of us knows when God is going to insert a turning point into our story, steering our future in an entirely different direction than anything we could have imagined.

> None of us knows when God is going to insert a turning point into our story.

PAUSE TO PONDER

Have you ever faced a crossroad where God led you in an unexpected direction? How did the events shape your understanding of God's greater purpose for your life?

The Promise

Reread Genesis 17:4-8 printed below, which is copied from the ESV Bible translation.

"Behold, my covenant is with you, and you shall be the father of a multitude of nations. No longer shall your name be called Abram, but your name shall be Abraham, for I have made you the father of a multitude of nations. I will make you exceedingly fruitful, and I will make you into nations, and kings shall come from you. And I will establish my covenant between me and you and your offspring after you . . . for an everlasting covenant, to be God to you and to your offspring after you. And I will give to you and to your offspring after you the land of your sojournings, all the land of Canaan, for an everlasting possession, and I will be their God."

Based on the passage you just read, complete the table as follows. In the first column, list all persons or groups of people mentioned in the text, except for God and Abraham. In the second column, indicate the number of times each group is mentioned. Lastly, using the instructions in the third column, go back and mark each group in the text as indicated.

Persons/people (other than God and Abraham)	Mentioned how many times?	Marking the text
		Place circle around each
		Place box around each
		Underline each

Look carefully once more at the text, paying particular attention to the words you marked. In the margin, record anything interesting that you notice.

A Promise within a Promise

Previously, you learned how repetition in Scripture can serve to emphasize a particular point the author wants to make. In this case, the repeated phrases appear to be focusing our attention on something else. Take a look.

> Complete the following sentences based on the passage you just studied.
>
> (1x) You shall be the father of a multitude of _____.
>
> (2x) I have made you the father of a multitude of _____.
>
> (3x) I will make you exceedingly fruitful, and I will make you into _____, and _____ shall come from you.
>
> (1x) I will establish my covenant between me and you and your _____ after you.
>
> (2x) To be God to you and to your _____ after you.
>
> (3x) I will give to you and to your _____ after you.

Not once, but three times, God repeats His promise to Abraham and then does the same thing regarding Abraham's offspring.

> Examine the fill-ins you completed in the previous question. What does the author slip into the middle? Who do you suppose this reference may be pointing to?

The promise that "kings shall come from you" certainly points to earthly kings—namely, the future nation of Israel's succession of kings. However, this Scripture also foreshadows someone else—namely, the future King of the world, who is Jesus Christ. For modern day readers of the Bible, the significance of the word "Christ" is not so obvious. In Old Testament times, kings were anointed with oil, and the word "anointed" became synonymous with "king." In the New Testament, the word *Christos* in Greek, Christ in English, literally means "Anointed One"—that is, the King.

Throughout the Old Testament, God gave visions to various prophets concerning the future kingdom of God and His coming King. Let's take a look.

> Read Daniel 7:13-14 and contrast all the ways the kingdom in Daniel's vision is unlike any other kingdom on earth.

A Difficult Choice

Let's now return to Hagar's story to see what all of this might mean for her and her son Ishmael. Hagar had watched her son grow into a young man. For thirteen years, he was considered to be the child God promised to Abraham. This assumption is made evident when we read that both Abraham and Sarah were stunned to discover they would have a son in their old age. Imagine what Hagar might have been thinking at this point. *Will Ishmael be replaced? What does this mean for our future?* Surely the memory of her painful past would come flooding back. Now she learns her son is not the fulfillment of God's promise to Abraham. And yet, we read the beautiful assurance that Ishmael was included in God's covenant.

> Try to imagine yourself in Hagar's sandals. If you were given a choice, which would you choose? (1) That Ishmael would remain Abraham's sole heir, thereby ensuring you and your son would enjoy an abundance of earthly protection and benefits; or (2) to forfeit any assurance of earthly security, but know that you are included in God's "everlasting covenant, to be God to you and to your offspring after you" (Gen. 17:7). Explain your choice.

"Now faith is the assurance of things hoped for, the conviction of things not seen." —Hebrews 11:1

PAUSE TO PONDER

Think of a time when you felt rejected, replaced, or forgotten. How can you relate to Hagar?

Looking back, can you see God's hand in the midst of your situation? If so, complete the following sentence.

When I was _____ [approximate age(s)], I felt rejected, replaced, or forgotten when _____ _____ [describe the situation].

But God _____ _____ [describe how God revealed Himself, or protected or comforted you, or used the events for good].

If you are unable to recognize God's presence in the situation, spend some time this week in prayer and ask God to help you see the ways He intervened or used the situation to accomplish something positive. Perhaps He is using the situation to help you see yourself as He sees you: as His beloved child. When you are ready, go back and complete the fill-in sentence as God enables you.

Note: It may be that the same scenario comes to your mind that you recorded in a similar question previously in the study. If possible, try to think of a different situation that may apply to each question. The application will become clearer as we progress through the study. If the wounds are very recent or too painful, know that your heavenly Father desires to lead you to a place of restoration. Bring your heartache to Him in prayer and then inquire if He wants you to share your situation with a counselor, your pastor, or a trusted friend.

Truly, we are blessed to be able to hold in our hands God's precious promises: the Word of God. Hagar did not have such a gift. She was given the assurance of neither of the choices presented earlier. Option one (of Ishmael remaining Abraham's sole heir) would all but disappear the moment Isaac was born. Option two (the promise of God's everlasting presence) would require additional revelation from God that would not arrive until the ultimate Promised Child—that is, Jesus—entered the world. However, Hagar had what few would ever experience in this life: a face-to-face encounter with the Living God. Still, Hagar had a choice to make: whether or not to believe that the "God Who Sees Me" would still be there for her—no matter what.

·······································Your Turn ·····································

Is there anything in this life that you would hesitate to give up if God asked you to? Have you reached the point in your life where you seek God's presence more than His blessings? Explain.

Regardless of where you are, list one or two practical steps you will take this week to nurture your walk with God. In the margin, write a prayer of commitment.

DAY THREE
Counting Your Blessings

When I was halfway through seminary, I was laid off from my job. I worked at a city-owned airport and had the least seniority in my department. Not once, but three times, I was laid off from the same position. Finally, I was offered a permanent position at the same airport, but it was a third less pay and a terrible fit. I was miserable.

There Is No "Plan B"

One weekend, I went away to spend some time with the Lord to seek His counsel. *God, should I look for another job—again? Do You want me to go back to doing contract work?* I had so many questions. *Will I have to quit seminary?* I wanted to cry out, *I'm single, remember? I have bills and rent and tuition to pay. I'm running out of options, Lord!* After two days of prayer, I woke the following morning with a clear direction from the Lord. Actually, it was more of a gentle admonishment. I felt the Lord say to me, "You keep looking for Plan B—a new job or other income. There is no Plan B . . . or C . . . or D. There is no other plan but Me. Trust Me." It was then that I realized what God was telling me to do: quit my job and enter seminary full-time. I nearly laughed out loud. *Seriously, Lord?*

"Trust Me. I will take care of you."

I returned home and asked my Bible study group and other close friends to pray. For six weeks, we prayed. During that time, I examined my budget, my reserves, even my retirement fund. I put everything on the table, asking God to help me be certain of what I believed He wanted me to do. I calculated how large a course load I could handle each term, how many classes I needed to complete, and how soon I might be able to graduate. *If I work really hard, Lord willing, I could graduate in fourteen months.* It suddenly seemed so close that I actually wept. I still had no idea where the funds would come from, but at the end of six weeks, my prayer partners confirmed what God was asking me to do. So, just eight months after securing a permanent government job complete with benefits and a pension, I quit and enrolled in seminary full-time.

And God kept His promise.

Reread Genesis 17:15–22.

When God tells Abraham that Sarah will soon give birth to a son, Abraham cannot help but laugh. While Abraham and Sarah had spent thirteen years setting up Plan B, that day Abraham discovered "there is no other plan but Me."

> "If we are faithless, he remains faithful—for he cannot deny himself."
> —2 Timothy 2:13

PAUSE TO PONDER

Read 2 Timothy 2:13 in the margin, then answer the questions that follow.

Reflect on a time when you stepped outside God's boundaries, yet looking back, you can see God's faithfulness toward you.

List all of the ways God proved Himself faithful.

What impact did this have on your relationship with God?

Jesus tells us, "With man this is impossible, but with God all things are possible." —Matthew 19:26

Despite Abraham and Sarah's faults and failures, God kept His promise. Just as God changed Abram's name to Abraham to reflect his expanded role in God's plan (Abram means "exalted father," whereas Abraham means "father of a multitude"), God also changed Sarah's name from Sarai (my princess) to Sarah (princess)[3], when He declared that she, along with Abraham, would parent a "multitude of nations." However, for the past thirteen years, Abraham had enjoyed watching his son Ishmael grow into a young man, having pegged all of his hopes on this child, his only son.

Using your own words, rewrite what Abraham asks of God in Genesis 17:18.

What can you infer about Abraham's relationship to Ishmael at this point?

Try to imagine the anguish behind Abraham's plea. What fears seem to have surfaced in Abraham concerning his son Ishmael now that the true promised child would soon be born?

God did not forget Ishmael. Depending on how the text in verse 19 is translated, the passage can be misunderstood. The original Hebrew word commonly translated "no" in verse 19 is not negative in tone, but rather explicative.[4] The word is *abal*, which relates to truth. Its general meaning is "verily," and it may also be translated as "truly" or "nevertheless."[5] While Ishmael would not be the bearer of God's covenant, *nevertheless*, he would be among those who were welcome to become sharers in it.

One commentary author writes, "Abraham expresses his anticipation of an indefinite neglect of Ishmael, which was painful to his parental heart. He asks for him, therefore, a life from God in the highest sense. Since Abraham, according to [Genesis] 16, actually fell into the erroneous expectation, that the promise of God to him would be fulfilled in Ishmael, and since there is no record of any divine correction of his error in the meantime, the new revelation from God could only so be introduced when [Abraham] begins to be [troubled] about Ishmael."[6]

Recall from memory the meaning of Ishmael's name: _____.

What words of comfort does God use to reassure Abraham in Genesis 17:20a?

List every promise God makes concerning Ishmael in verse 20.

The Short List

Last week, we learned that Ishmael is among a very select group of people personally named by God before they were born. Today, we will discover that Ishmael is also included in yet another exclusive list. While all of God's people are inherently blessed by belonging to Him,[7] there are nonetheless a handful of references in the Old Testament[8] that specifically express God's blessing on a particular person, couple, or family.

Choose at least five of the following passages to read in your Bible. Then list the names of the person(s) blessed by God and how Scripture describes the blessing.

Scripture reference	Person(s) blessed by God	How were they blessed?
Genesis 1:27–28		
Genesis 9:1		
Genesis 12:1–2		
Genesis 17:15–16		
Genesis 17:20		
Genesis 26:3–4 (also 25:11)		
Genesis 35:9–11		
1 Chronicles 26:4–5		
Job 42:12–13, 16		

What common thread do you notice among these blessings?

How does God's promise to Hagar in Genesis 16:10 parallel the blessings in the list?

Look ahead to Genesis 49:28. How does God's blessing on Ishmael in Genesis 17:20 parallel the blessing that would one day be experienced by Isaac's future son, Jacob?

 What conclusions can you draw?

Things Are Not Always as They Seem

Based on what you know up to this point of Hagar's story, where would you place an X on this line concerning Hagar?

highly favored by God _____ not at all favored by God

Now, imagine that you are Hagar. If, during each of the following periods of time, you were asked whether you felt favored by God, where would you place an X?

When Hagar finds herself used, abused, pregnant, and alone in the desert:

highly favored by God _____ not at all favored by God

As the mother of Abraham's only son, Ishmael, who is now thirteen years old (prior to God appearing to Abraham in Genesis 17:1):

highly favored by God _____ not at all favored by God

After learning that God announced to Abraham that Sarah will soon give birth to a son:

highly favored by God _____ not at all favored by God

 Consider your responses; what insights did you gain from this exercise?

Your marks may be all over the place. Whenever we try to assess God's favor toward us based on our feelings or circumstances, we are viewing God through broken, shifting lenses. As a result, we run the risk of believing God to be unpredictable, untrustworthy, or even unloving—all of which are a great offense to His character. What Hagar could not have known was that the "God Who Sees Me" was orchestrating a glorious plan precisely with her, and countless others, on His mind.

In the same way, God is working Behind the Seen in your life. Oh, I can hardly wait until we reach the end of the study. By then, if not before, you will see that God's glorious plan, which He set in motion before the beginning of time, is being orchestrated precisely with you in mind.

PAUSE TO PONDER

Look up the following passages.

Romans 8:31–32

Colossians 1:16–17

How can these Scriptures encourage you when you allow circumstances to foster doubt or discouragement in your heart?

Earthly Blessings

Read Psalm 41:1–3 and 112:1–3. What earthly benefits does the psalmist expect will be experienced by those who follow God? List them below.

Of the earthly benefits you listed, is there one you personally long for? If so, write it down.

Of all the earthly benefits described in these passages, is there one you feel (or have felt in the past) that God is holding back from you? If so, which one?

Read Genesis 3:1–5. How does the temptation to believe God is withholding something from us mirror Satan's temptation of Eve in Genesis 3:5?

Posterity and prosperity are merely temporal and physical; the greatest blessings are eternal and spiritual.

Everlasting Promises

Read the statement in the margin. Do you agree? Why or why not?

Do you recall from Day One of this week's lesson how many times God describes His covenant with Abraham as "everlasting"? (If not, glance back at page 84.)

Reread Genesis 17:7-8. What specific promise does God repeat after He uses the word "everlasting" in each verse?

While God would surely keep His promises to bless Abraham and Sarah, as well as Hagar, the greatest of these promises is God's assurance that "I will be their God." Can children and wealth last forever? Although children, land, and wealth in the Old Testament were certainly blessings given by God to enjoy, they served an even greater purpose. God's gifts to His people bring glory to God by making His name known as the One who protects and blesses His people—a people through whom the promised Savior of the world would one day come. Only when we reach the New Testament are the infinitely more glorious and "everlasting" blessings that await God's people clearly revealed.

Read Matthew 5:3-12; then complete the table.

In the second column, describe each group of persons that Jesus calls blessed.

In the last column, record how they are blessed.

Scripture reference	Person(s) blessed by God	How are they blessed? (What does Jesus promise them?)
Verse 3		
Verse 4		
Verse 5		
Verse 6		

Verse 7		
Verse 8		
Verse 9		
Verse 10		
Verse 11–12	[Hint: look for repeated words]	

······················Your Turn ·····························

Reflect on Jesus's promises in Matthew 5:3–12. Which promises do you personally long for the most?

Compare your answer to this question with your answers in the Earthly Blessings section on page 99. If you could be granted only one or the other, which would you choose? Why?

Write a prayer of thanksgiving for God's provision and faithfulness in the margin.

DAY FOUR
Believing in God's Faithfulness

Perhaps nowhere else in the Bible are the problems of mankind so succinctly portrayed than in the book of Malachi, the last book in the Old Testament. The days of Malachi mirror much of what we see in our world today. Priests were corrupt, divorce was rampant, worship was lifeless, social justice was being ignored, and giving financially to God's work was being neglected. In a nutshell, the hearts of God's people had grown cold.

Nevertheless, the book is most often quoted as an object lesson for giving. "Bring the full tithe into the storehouse, that there may be food in my house. And thereby put me to the test, says the LORD of hosts, if I will not open the windows of heaven for you and pour down for you a blessing until there is no more need" (Mal. 3:10).

PAUSE TO PONDER

> Reread the third sentence in the introduction to today's lesson. Which description of the days of Malachi grieves your heart the most? Why?

Godly Offspring

The book of Malachi also provides a wonderful opportunity to gain a deeper understanding of why a holy God could not allow Ishmael, through no fault of his own, to take the place of the child of promise.

Read Malachi 2:15. According to this Scripture, what is God looking for?

Reread Genesis 17:15, 19. How does God describe Sarah to Abraham during their conversation?

Since Abraham knew perfectly well who Sarah was, why do you think God pointed out her relationship to Abraham, not once, but twice?

How do the following Scriptures, taken from the first and last books of the Old Testament, shed light on why God would choose Isaac rather than Ishmael as the one through whom God would establish His covenant?

Genesis 2:24

Malachi 2:14–16

God is holy. His promise to deliver mankind from its fallen condition hinges on providing a Savior. Because God Himself is a witness to the marriage covenant as revealed in the verses we just read, He could not allow the violation of that covenant to be the means through which He would fulfill His promise.

What eternal promise does God make to Abraham concerning Himself in Genesis 17? (If you do not remember, glance back at page 100.)

To use Ishmael, who was born of man's own efforts, as the lineage through whom the Christ would ultimately come denies God's power, authority, and offer of salvation. If we could save ourselves by our own efforts, we would not need a Savior. By God's grace, a Savior would one day come—but every step toward that end would be ordained by God, not man.

If we could save ourselves by our own efforts, we would not need a Savior.

PAUSE TO PONDER

> Describe a time when you tried to run ahead of God's timing or turned aside from God's plan. What were the results?

God's Covenant

Read Genesis 17:12–14 and 23–27; then answer the questions that follow.

List everyone God includes in the covenant. Be specific.

How many times does the author specify the inclusion of slaves who are members of Abraham's household, whether bought from a foreigner or born in his house (i.e., children born to foreign slaves)?

Do you think the repetition is significant? Why or why not?

List every male included in the covenant who was neither a slave nor born of a slave. What does this reveal about God's heart and intentions for those outside Abraham's immediate family?

Except for Abraham himself, every male circumcised at this time would have been either a slave or born of a slave. Even Ishmael, although Abraham's son, was born of a slave.

How many times is the circumcision of Ishmael specifically mentioned?

How does this shed further light on God's purpose for sending Hagar back to Sarah in Genesis 16:9?

Walking in the Footsteps of Abraham, the Father of Faith

Read Romans 4:11-12, 16-17. Who are Abraham's offspring according to these verses?

Are there any people who are born in a place, or time, or raised in a religion, or subject to any natural condition or external circumstance that disqualifies them from sharing the faith of Abraham? Explain your response.

Just imagine if God had not sought out Hagar when she ran away into the desert or if Hagar had not obeyed God by returning to Sarah. Truly, it was God's kindness that pursued Hagar into the desert. It was His great love for her and her unborn son that compelled Him to send Hagar back. If He had not, she and Ishmael would have missed being included in God's holy covenant!

PAUSE TO PONDER

Is there someone in your life whom you are tempted to believe is outside of God's reach? If so, take some time right now and ask God if perhaps you have been placed in that person's life for a reason. Respond as God leads you.

Command Your Children to "Keep the Way of the Lord"

Read Genesis 18:1-5, 16-19. (Optional: Read Genesis 18:1-19 all the way through.)
Write out Genesis 18:19 below.

Compare and contrast Genesis 17:9-10 with Genesis 18:19. Describe Abraham's
responsibility in each passage and the persons involved.

What else can you discover in these passages?

You may have noticed that God used a different word to refer to Abraham's
children in Genesis 18. In Genesis 17, God spoke specifically of Abraham's offspring,
descendants, or "seed" (depending on which Bible translation you use), in relation
to God's covenant plan. However, in Genesis 18:19, God used a different Hebrew
word, *banay*, which is the plural form of "son" to refer to Abraham's immediate
children (or family).

When the Lord describes Abraham as being chosen by Him to "command his
children . . . to keep the way of the LORD," who are the children of Abraham at
this point and their ages?

It is important to note that the word *command* in verse 19 is in an imperfect form
in Hebrew, which means it does not relate as much to a particular time (past,
present, or future) as to the unfolding of an ongoing activity. Further, because the
Lord is not speaking directly to Abraham, but rather is describing His relationship
with Abraham to His two companions, these facts suggest that Abraham has been
engaged in this activity (i.e., teaching his children, that is, Ishmael, to "keep the
way of the LORD") all along.

. . . And [Command] Your Household

When God commanded Abraham to obey the covenant of circumcision, Abraham
set himself up as the example to follow even though he was already ninety-nine
years old. The text says that Abraham and his son Ishmael were circumcised the

very same day the command was given. Following Abraham's example, all the other men and boys underwent the procedure as well. According to Genesis 14:14, we can estimate that there were hundreds—if not thousands—in his household. That is quite an undertaking! However, based on what we learned from Genesis 18:19, we can reasonably infer that for the past twenty or more years, Abraham had been teaching the people in his household to trust in God. Therefore, by the time God's command was given, it appears to have been met with little to no resistance, attesting to Abraham's faithfulness in leading his people just as God was leading Abraham.[9]

Where the Eyes Wander, the Feet Will Follow

In Day One of this week's lesson, we examined Abraham's walk with God, starting from when Abraham was seventy-five years old. We know that by the time Ishmael was born, Abraham had already been walking with God for roughly eleven years. This means that Ishmael would have heard amazing stories from both his mother and father, who each experienced miraculous personal encounters with God before Ishmael was born. Just imagine all of the firsthand accounts of God's love, protection, and faithfulness that Ishmael would have heard growing up.

Then, suddenly, when Ishmael was thirteen years old, rumors of a "new" promised child spread through the camp. I do not know about you, but I would expect Scripture to lead right into a detailed account of all the preparations being made in anticipation of the child's birth as well as the excitement, anxiety, and even conflict building within the camp. Instead, without warning, the story is abruptly placed on hold. As a matter of fact, the account of Isaac's impending birth remains on hold for a full two and a half chapters. Let's see if we can find out why.

First, we need to do some backtracking.

Think back to Week One. Who accompanied Abraham and Sarah when they first set out for the land of Canaan? (For a hint, glance back at Genesis 12:4.)

Please read Genesis 13:5–15; then answer the questions that follow.

Why did Lot separate from his uncle?

Where did Lot eventually settle, according to verse 12?

Read Genesis 13:10-11 and 13:14-15; then answer the questions that follow.

Compare the two passages. What observations can you make?

Who or what was guiding Lot's decisions?

Who or what was guiding Abraham's?

"Trust in the LORD with all your heart,
    and do not lean on your own understanding.
In all your ways acknowledge him,
    and he will make straight your paths.
Be not wise in your own eyes;
    fear the LORD, and turn away from evil." —Proverbs 3:5–7

Spend a few moments meditating on Proverbs 3:5-7 above. Where would you place an X on the lines below?

Lot walked by sight _____ Lot walked by faith

Abraham walked by sight _____ Abraham walked by faith

PAUSE TO PONDER

How about you? Where would you place an X on the line below?

I walk by sight _____ I walk by faith

Judgment versus Mercy

Optional: Read Genesis 14:8–16.

Genesis 14 reveals that Abraham not only knew Lot had settled in Sodom, but that Abraham was willing to risk his own life to save him when enemies attacked. Please keep this in mind as we move forward.

Read Genesis 18:20–33. Describe Abraham's response to the Lord's impending judgment.

What might be underlying Abraham's fears, according to what you recently read in Genesis 13?

Reflect on the exchange between God and Abraham in Genesis 18:20–33, then read each of the two statements below. Which one do you find yourself agreeing with most? Mark your response by placing an X on the line below.

God is just (He is willing to withhold mercy in order to enact judgment).

God is merciful (He is willing to withhold judgment in order to extend mercy).

God is just _____ God is merciful

Explain your response.

You and I live in a fallen world. We are mortal, sinful, and for the most part, wounded. All of these realities will inevitably influence our view of God in either one direction or the other. However, the Bible teaches that God is both a God of justice and a God of mercy. He is also infinite, having no beginning and no end; therefore, He cannot be more just than He is merciful or more merciful than He is just. It is a staggering, yet precious, truth that the infinite justice and infinite mercy of God exist together in perfect harmony. Try to imagine: a just God without mercy would be a terror; a merciful God without justice would be a tragedy. Either way, we would all suffer.

Think back on a time you did something that you know grieved God. With this situation in mind, how did you view God? Where would you place an X on the line below?

God is just _____ God is merciful

Compare your response above to the same question you answered previously. Did it change? Share your thoughts.

In what ways have you been affected by holding on to an inaccurate view of God?

In the margin, write a prayer of confession as God leads you.

DAY FIVE
The Power of Intercessory Prayer

I will never forget the day: September 5, 2014. It was three weeks before I was to travel across the country to deliver a keynote address at a pregnancy center banquet. For the previous two months, I had been struggling with the sober message God put on my heart. I even contacted the director to share with her the challenging message I planned to deliver. I reasoned that if she wanted to back out of our contract, this was her chance. Her response? "Bring it on." She went on to explain that the message was precisely what the people in that spiritually dark region needed to hear. Her reply confirmed God's message. Encouraged, I pressed ahead. However, as the date approached, oppression set in. At first, I thought it was the familiar struggles of self-doubt and fear.

I was wrong.

A Dark Night of the Soul

I had heard of the expression "dark night of the soul," and apparently I was about to find out exactly what it meant. I experienced a spiritual attack unlike anything I had ever known. For three days and two nights, I could not feel God's presence.

I am not referring to the periodic times when God seems distant. No. It was more than that. God had hidden from me any ability to sense His presence. It felt as if the Holy Spirit had been ripped from my soul, and because my soul is knitted to His Spirit, it felt as if my own soul had been torn from my body.

I implored my church family to pray, and a pastor friend sent me a link to a song I had never heard before. It was called *Never Alone* by Barlow Girl. God used the simple, but powerful, lyrics of that song to carry me as I clung desperately to the truth of His Word: He promises never to leave me or forsake me. For three tormented days, I had nothing to hold on to except the truth of God's Word. I could not feel Him. I could not sense Him. It felt as if my entire being had been swallowed up in darkness, but I had to trust that He was still there. I had no choice except to stand on His Word alone: He will never leave me or forsake me.

When God finally delivered me, I thought I would never see any good from having gone through such torment. Thankfully, when the night of the banquet arrived, God used the message and His Word for His glory and good purposes. Had it not been for the faithful saints who bathed me, and the event, in prayer, the outcome may have been very different.

A few weeks later, I wrote the following in my journal: *Father, thank You for the days of oppression I suffered a few weeks ago. It was painful and confusing at the time, but I've come through it—by Your grace and the precious prayers of Your saints—stronger in faith, love, and worship than I've ever been before. I spent the afternoon yesterday at the beach listening to worship music on my iPod and could not help but dance! Thank You, God, for such a precious time praising You. Please do not let this worship "high" diminish, but rather help me to fan it into a roaring flame....*

God continues to answer my prayer.

> I had to trust that He was still there. I had no choice except to stand on His Word alone: He will never leave me or forsake me.

PAUSE TO PONDER

Think of a time you experienced the power of intercessory prayer. How did God move? How did the experience impact your relationship with God?

Living Among the Ungodly

Read Genesis 19:1-3.

How does Lot's treatment of the visitors mirror the conduct of Abraham in Genesis 18:1-5?

If this was the only thing you knew about Lot, how might you describe his character?

Read Genesis 19:4–29.

Rewrite verse 4 exactly as it appears in your Bible.

Has the author left any doubt as to whether there was even one man in the city who was not part of the brazen mob surrounding Lot's house? Would this include, then, the men pledged to marry Lot's daughters?

Contrast the mob's intentions with Lot's. Why do you suppose Lot "pressed [the visitors] strongly" to come under his roof? What does this reveal about Lot's awareness of the dangers in his city?

Choose Your Friends Wisely

In Genesis 13, when the herdsmen of Abraham and Lot clashed over the needs of their ever-increasing flocks and herds, Abraham tried to reason with Lot, appealing to the fact that they were relatives (Gen. 13:8). In Genesis 19:7, Lot likewise tries to reason with the violent mob by calling them "brothers."[10] In both passages, the root Hebrew word is identical: *ash* meaning "brother."

List two or three reasons that may have compelled Lot to appeal to the men of Sodom as brothers.

Read the following passages and record any insights you gain.

2 Corinthians 6:14, 17

2 Peter 2:7–8

"And he believed the LORD, and he counted it to him as righteousness."

—Genesis 15:6

Scripture tells us that Lot was a righteous, though tormented, man. Given his many poor choices, fears, and reckless judgment—even endangering his own children in an irrational moment of panic—it is difficult to feel sympathy for him, much less think of him as righteous. Yet Scripture does not lie.

Read Genesis 15:6 in the margin. What must occur for God to count (or regard) someone as righteous, according to this verse?

Is it possible for someone who still makes mistakes, even someone like Lot, to be regarded by God as righteous? Explain.

Consider your answer to the previous question. Are you encouraged? Why or why not?

Genesis 13:10–11 gives us some insight as to what first attracted Lot to the region. However, why Lot would choose to stay in a city and live among people whose very lives caused him such grief is difficult to discern.

List as many possibilities as you can think of that may have been behind Lot's decision to stay in Sodom.

Perhaps you listed pride, or fear, or position. In Old Testament times, a person "sitting in the gate," as we read of Lot in Genesis 19:1, signified someone who had authority in that city.[11] Maybe Lot caved in to pressure from his wife. Scripture gives no indication that Lot was married until he was already living in Sodom. His wife's inability not to look back at the city when God destroyed it suggests her heart was attached to Sodom.

One thing is clear: Lot and his tiny family were living in a place and among people who were "great sinners against the LORD" (Gen. 13:13). While Lot could have sought out nearby relatives to marry his daughters, which was customary, he instead chose to stay put. Separated from his relatives and having lost all credibility (even his future sons-in-law did not believe him), he did not stand a chance.

But God . . .

Reread Genesis 19:16. When it came time to escape the impending destruction of the city, how did Lot respond? What did God do and why?

According to Genesis 19:29, who did God remember and who did God rescue as a result?

How do the following verses contribute to your understanding of God's activity in Genesis 19?

Proverbs 15:29

James 5:16

1 Peter 3:12

"For the eyes of the Lord are on the righteous, and his ears are open to their prayer." —1 Peter 3:12a

Clinging to Your Faith in a World That Is Falling Apart

Reread Genesis 19:27–28. What did Abraham see? What assurance did he have that the Lord had answered his unspoken plea in Genesis 18:23 to protect his nephew Lot?

"Will you indeed sweep away the righteous with the wicked?"
—Genesis 18:23

In Genesis 15:6, we are told that Abraham "believed the Lord" when the Lord promised him he would be the father of children as numerous as the stars. About twenty-five years later, Abraham found himself standing all alone, gazing down at the smoking inferno of the once-thriving cities where his beloved nephew lived. If God was faithful to His Word (which He always is), Abraham would have realized right then that there had not been even ten righteous persons in the whole region. Surely Abraham was grieved not knowing what happened to Lot, leaving him with nothing to cling to but his faith in who God is: "Far be it from you to do such a thing, to put the righteous to death with the wicked, so that the righteous fare as the wicked! Far be that from you! Shall not the Judge of all the earth do what is just?" (Gen. 18:25).

....Your Turn..

Is there an "unknown" that you or someone you love is struggling with right now? Perhaps an unknown diagnosis? A wayward child? A non-committed or threatened relationship? A sudden job loss?

How might God use this time of wrestling with an "unknown" for good?

Read Romans 8:26–28. What would it look like to trust God in this situation? Write your response in the form of a prayer in the margin.

Lesson Summary

What Scripture, statement, or thought was most significant to you this week? Write it down and then reword it into a prayer of response to God.

There is a worship song that I think wonderfully captures the heart of this week's lesson. It is called "The Same Love" by Paul Baloche. Perhaps you will enjoy it as well.

Reminder: If you have not completed the Pause to Ponder section on page 93, please go back and complete it now.

Notes

[1] See Matthew 4:19, 9:9; Mark 1:17, 2:14; Luke 5:27; and John 1:43.

[2] J. D. Currid, *A Study Commentary on Genesis*, vol. 1, *Genesis 1:1–25:18* (Darlington, England: Evangelical Press, 2003), 311.

[3] W. Smith, "Sarah," in *Smith's Bible Dictionary* (Nashville: Thomas Nelson, 1986), Logos edition.

[4] Most translations (NET, NCV, NASB, CEV, CEB, ASV, ESV, NLT, NKJV, and HCSB) use "no" or "no, but." Exceptions include the KJV and YLT, which are silent, and the NIV, which translates it as "yes."

[5] R. L. Thomas, *New American Standard Hebrew-Aramaic and Greek Dictionaries: Updated Edition* (Anaheim: Foundation Publications, 1998).

[6] J. P. Lange et al., *A Commentary on the Holy Scriptures: Genesis* (Bellingham, WA: Logos Bible Software, 2008), 425.

[7] There are many Old Testament references relating to God's blessing of his covenant people, the Israelites, as a whole. Examples include Numbers 22:12; Deuteronomy 7:12–14, 15:4; Psalm 33:12, 144:15; and Isaiah 30:18. The New Testament, likewise, teaches of God's blessing through Christ for both Jews and Gentiles. See Ephesians 1:3 and 3:6.

[8] Absent from this list is Judges 13:24, which does not state specifically how Samson was blessed, along with three references in the New Testament: Mary in Luke 1:42, Peter in Matthew 16:17, and the disciples in Luke 24:50.

[9] Because slaves had no other choice but to obey, the silence of Scripture regarding the response of the men in Abraham's household did not rule out that there may have been some who obeyed externally but resisted the command in their hearts. However, as we know from Hagar's story, slaves could have resorted to running away. The fact that there was no protest, rebellion, or runaway slaves mentioned in the text gives weight to the interpretation that opposition to the command was little to none. (This is not to say, of course, that the participants would have looked forward to the procedure itself.)

[10] Note: The NIV translation replaces the Hebrew word "brothers" in this verse with "friends."

[11] See Deuteronomy 21:19 and Joshua 20:4.

TRUSTING IN
GOD'S
PROTECTION

SEVERAL YEARS HAVE PASSED. ALTHOUGH HAGAR AND Ishmael are established members of Abraham's covenant community, all of that is about to change. When the unimaginable strikes, witness the depths of God's mercy as He not only orchestrates His protection over Hagar and Ishmael, but also opens Hagar's eyes to His far greater plans for her life.

DAY ONE
Give God All the Broken Pieces

Last week, we examined the events in Genesis 18 and 19. This week, we will discover why those events, along with those in Genesis 20, are placed where they are. Only then can we dive into Genesis 21, where we will pick up the story of the birth of Isaac, the child of promise.

Let's get started.

A Redeemed Past

During my seminary studies, I was fascinated by the story of a missionary named Mary Slessor, whose heart compelled her to risk even her life to rescue abandoned infants in the jungles of Africa. But it was not Mary's passion that intrigued me so much as it was her painful childhood journey that prepared her for God's call.

Mary Slessor was born in 1848 into an abusive home in the slums of Scotland.[1] As a small child, Mary watched helplessly as her alcoholic father routinely battered her mother. When Mary was just seven years old, she began taunting her father when he arrived home drunk in an effort to deflect his rage. She would often tire him out by racing through the house as he tried to catch her. Mary was petite for her age and frequently, but not always, succeeded in escaping his wrath.

A few years later, Mary was sent to work at the local mill, where she worked and went to school twelve hours a day. In her precious spare time, Mary started a Bible study for street children. No sooner had she begun, however, than a local bully began threatening the group. Though younger and smaller than he, Mary stood her ground, and in an ironic twist, the bully became her group's most loyal guardian and protector.

When Mary was twenty-seven, she came to admire the work of missionary David Livingstone. Desiring to follow in his footsteps, Mary set her sights on Africa at a time when it was unheard-of for single women to enter the mission field. Upon arriving, Mary was shocked to discover hundreds of slain or abandoned twin babies and their outcast mothers, rejected because the villagers believed that twins were conceived by the devil. Filled with compassion and the truth of God's Word, Mary began rescuing the children, caring for the women, and introducing God's love to the people. Her years of enduring childhood abuse, bullies, and threats prepared this petite, fiery redhead to confront even the most imposing of African chiefs—earning both their respect and the freedom to minister to their women and children.

Like Mary, each of us, with all of our triumphs and failures, joys and heartbreaks, scars and all, has been given an opportunity to make a difference in our world. Let us never underestimate what God can do with a life solely surrendered to Him.

> Each of us has been given an opportunity to make a difference in our world. Never underestimate what God can do with a life solely surrendered to Him.

PAUSE TO PONDER

> What about Mary Slessor's story stood out to you the most? Why do you suppose it captured your attention?

Misplaced Fear

Read all of Genesis 20; then answer the questions that follow.

Who was Abimelech afraid of?

Who was Abraham afraid of?

What assumption did Abraham make concerning the king and his people's view of God?

What was Abraham's underlying fear, and how might it have tainted his judgment?

Let's pause here a moment and try to imagine what it must have been like for Sarah. This is now the second time Scripture records that Abraham was willing to put his wife at risk to save his own neck (the first time was when Sarah was taken by Egypt's Pharaoh, as recorded in Genesis 12:11–15). While Christians revere Abraham as our "father of faith,"[2] here we are reminded that even the godly are not immune to fears and failures.

How might Abraham's decision to conceal that Sarah was his wife have affected Sarah's sense of self-worth?

Do you suppose these experiences may have had an influence on Sarah's treatment of Hagar? Share your thoughts.

PAUSE TO PONDER

> When entering an unfamiliar place or situation, how can past hurts or fears affect your ability to see clearly?

Most scholars agree that Abimelech, which means "father of the king," is actually a title, not a name. Abimelech is used as the "name of several Philistine kings . . . like that of Pharaoh among the Egyptians and that of Caesar and Augustus among the Romans."[3]

In describing how the king addressed God, the author of Genesis used a Hebrew word with an emphatic (direct, spoken with strong emphasis) form of the word Lord (*Adonay*). Do you think this is significant? Why or why not?

How do the king's servants react upon hearing of the king's dream? How does this compare with Abraham's words in verse 11?

While Abraham's fear was misplaced, leading him to do things that even a foreign king knew "ought not to be done" (Gen. 20:9), Abimelech had no trouble recognizing the great danger he (along with his entire kingdom) had found himself in, despite the fact that the king himself was innocent of any wrongdoing.

The Fear of the Lord Is the Beginning of Wisdom

List every action God took according to Genesis 20. (Note: You do not need to include all that God said, unless it relays information about what God did.)

What reason does God give for preventing the king from approaching Sarah, according to verse 3?

How did the king respond to this message? What do his responses in verses 4–5 and 8–9 suggest about the king's beliefs and character?

"The fear of the LORD is the beginning of wisdom."

—Proverbs 9:10a

~~~ Consider the text carefully. Does it appear that God actually interfered with the king's free will? Explain.

Although the text does not offer specifics, God did intervene in the circumstances in order to temporarily keep the king away from Sarah. However, God never interfered with the king's free will; the king's initial intentions never changed until he was presented with new information. As a matter of fact, not only did God not interfere when the king took Sarah into his harem, but God gave the man a choice.

What were the king's options, as presented by God in the king's dream?

How else might the king have responded?

Even if the king dismissed the dream as coming from his own imagination, God is real, His Word is power, and His plans will prevail.

~~~ List all the reasons God may have had for shielding Sarah from Abimelech.

Sarah is now ninety years old. While we know from Scripture that Sarah was a beautiful woman (Gen. 12:11, 14), it is unlikely the king's actions were motivated by physical desire. In Old Testament times, it was common for kings to marry relatives of those with whom they sought an alliance (1 Kings 3:1; 2 Chron. 18:1). If God had allowed Sarah to remain with the king, regardless of the king's reasons for taking her, the child promised to Abraham and Sarah would never have been born. However, God's eternal agenda, established before the beginning of time,[4] culminating with the birth of the Savior of the world, could not be thwarted.

What gifts did the king give to Abraham and Sarah, according to Genesis 20:14–16?

It would have been very easy for the king to instruct his servants to send his gifts on the king's behalf. Instead, he not only took personal responsibility for the task, but he did something else.

What else did the king do? Be specific.

If it was unclear as to whether the king slept with Sarah before returning her to Abraham, what doubts might have arisen when Sarah ultimately gave birth to a son? Your list may include doubts concerning the child, Abraham and Sarah, or even God.

From the list you just made, which do you think would have the most serious consequences? Why?

The Hand of God

We learned in Genesis 20:18 that "the LORD had closed all the wombs of the house of Abimelech." When I read these words, I cannot help but think of Hagar. Since God Almighty has the power to open and close the womb, He certainly could have kept Hagar from conceiving Ishmael.

What reasons might God have had for allowing Hagar to conceive, based on what you know so far of Hagar's story?

In the same way God allowed a threatening famine to deliver Hagar from Egypt and its pagan gods (after all, God could have rained down manna from heaven), He also allowed Abraham and Sarah's misguided schemes to deliver into Hagar's arms a beloved son.

What else did Hagar gain as a result of having left Egypt and conceiving Ishmael? Circle one.

a husband   her freedom   a divine encounter   riches

PAUSE TO PONDER

Think back on the challenges you have faced
in your own life. How do you see them now?
Where would you place an X on the line below?

calamities _____ opportunities

How do you suppose God sees them? Where might He place an X
on the line below? If you are not sure, consider Mary Slessor's story
instead. How do you suppose God saw the challenges in her story?

calamities _____ opportunities

I do not know what you have been through, but I know from personal experience that life can be hard. Abortion, date rape, drug and alcohol abuse, spousal abuse, divorce . . . these are just some of the heartaches from my past. However, one thing I have learned: when we surrender our heartaches into God's hands, He is faithful to use them for His glory—and perhaps, just perhaps—He may open our eyes to what He is doing Behind the Seen. But even if He does not, He is still working, He is still holy, and He is still good.

Truly, it was the very hand of God that brought Hagar out of Egypt. It was He who enabled her to conceive a son, a gift from God and a blessing considered the highest honor in that time. It was God who provided for Hagar's protection, and He chose her to be the first to experience a miraculous encounter with the Angel of the Lord. It was God who pursued Hagar and spoke tenderly to her in the desert, promising to "multiply [her] offspring so that they cannot be numbered for multitude" (Gen. 16:10). Clearly, *El Roi* had been working Behind the Seen in Hagar's life all along . . . and her powerful story is just beginning to unfold.

> Even if we cannot see what God is doing, He is still working, He is still holy, and He is still good.

Your Turn

Think back on Mary Slessor's story at the beginning of today's lesson.

Is there someone in your past who abandoned you in some way? (Note: Abandonment can be physical separation, but it also includes the emotional pain of loneliness, abuse, or neglect.) If so, how might the experience be hindering you from fully trusting God for your future?

If you have suffered abandonment, have you placed it into God's hands for His use? If yes, how has He used it? Write a prayer of praise for what He has done.

If there is still a wound that requires healing, what needs to happen for you to give God all the broken pieces? Write a prayer of confession in the margin as God leads you. If you have never experienced this heartache, write a prayer of gratitude for God's protection in this area.

Day Two
Finding Refuge in God's Protection

Refresh your memory by rereading Genesis 15:4 and 18:9–14.

What new information does Abraham receive from the Lord in Genesis 18?

How many times does the Lord repeat this new information?

Then, this happened . . .

Briefly recount the events of Genesis 19:1–29.

And this . . .

Briefly recount the events of Genesis 20, being careful not to overlook verse 1.

Abraham has endured much in his elderly years: experiencing the birth of his beloved son Ishmael followed by the proclamation that Ishmael was not the child God promised; witnessing the destruction of Sodom and Gomorrah while fearing for the safety of his nephew Lot; packing up his entire camp, including hundreds if not thousands of people,[5] possessions, massive tents, and ever-multiplying flocks and herds, and trekking everything through the desert; then setting it up all over again, only to have his wife snatched up by the local king. So many years, so many trials . . . Meanwhile, God had made a promise, and the clock is ticking.

What's in a Name?

Read Genesis 21:1–7.

We discovered in Genesis 20 that God was willing to go to great lengths to protect Sarah from the king's intentions. However, perhaps it was not Sarah's reputation that was primarily at stake.

> Glance back at the questions on page 122. What did you list as being the most serious outcome if Scripture had not been clear that the king had not touched Sarah?

Whose reputation was ultimately at risk?

the king's   Sarah's   Abraham's   God's

What detail concerning the fulfillment of God's promise to give Abraham and Sarah a son does the author point out in Genesis 21:2? Do you think this is significant? Why or why not?

God does not need our affirmation or applause. If He is orchestrating events in order to protect His name in the eyes of man, it is because we are the ones who need to know He is faithful, trustworthy, and good. "The LORD visited Sarah *as he had said*, and the LORD did to Sarah *as he had promised*" (Gen. 21:1; emphasis mine).

Write Sarah's question as recorded in Genesis 21:7.

Try to imagine you are in the tent with Sarah. If you knew you could speak freely, how might you have responded?

> "The LORD visited Sarah *as he had said*, and the LORD did to Sarah *as he had promised.*" —Genesis 21:1; emphasis mine

It is not clear to whom Sarah was speaking (perhaps the midwife, or Abraham, or maybe herself, or everyone within earshot). Given the circumstances, it is reasonable to presume her question was rhetorical. Still, I can just picture someone in the tent bursting at the seams, wanting to respond, "Excuse me, my lady, but didn't you tell us that the Lord visited Abraham not that long ago and that He . . . well, promised precisely that?"

The truth is, we do not know all of the details, but this much we do know: Sarah's long-abandoned dream to have a child of her own actually came true. Perhaps Sarah is simply laughing. Again. After all, she is ninety years old and just gave birth. Right on time, by the way. I'd probably be laughing, too.

The Last Laugh

Read Genesis 21:8-10.

Let's get this straight. When Sarah laughs and God confronts her about it in Genesis 18, she denies it. When Sarah gives birth and anticipates that "everyone who hears will laugh," she rejoices. But when Sarah sees Hagar's son laughing, she's incensed. Apparently, *everyone's* laughter did not include Ishmael's. Happy one minute; incensed the next.

Okay. It was not really a minute later. Or even a day. Or a year, for that matter. Still, there does seem to be a pattern here. When life is going her way, all is well in the camp, but when it is not going so well, look out!

Let's try to put this into perspective. Hebrew children were normally weaned around the age of two to three years.[6] (Some scholars would put the age at three to four years old.[7]) We know that Ishmael was thirteen when the Lord announced to Abraham that Sarah would give birth to a son in a year's time. If Isaac was weaned between the ages of two and three years old, Ishmael would now already be sixteen or seventeen years of age.

> Carefully examine Genesis 21:9 in the margin. What does it say? What does it *not* say? Or, try to picture the scene in your mind based solely on what is written in the text. What do you see? What do you *not* see?

"But Sarah saw the son of Hagar the Egyptian, whom she had borne to Abraham, laughing." —Genesis 21:9

We do not know precisely what Ishmael was doing. This should be good reason enough for us to pause before making any conclusions.

DOES THE NEW TESTAMENT REJECT HAGAR?

The wording of Genesis 21:9 makes it unclear as to exactly what Ishmael was doing. When we add to that the difficult passage in the New Testament book of Galatians (the only other place this story appears in the entire Bible), the events seem even more curious.

Read Galatians 4:21–31.

On its surface, the apostle Paul seems to cast Hagar and Ishmael in a very disparaging light. However, the passage in Galatians, like any other portion of Scripture, can be misunderstood or, worse, misapplied without proper Biblical exegesis (a critical explanation or interpretation of a text). Let's pause and spend a few moments examining Paul's teaching in Galatians 4.

How does Paul describe his message according to the beginning of verse 24? Do you think this is important? Why or why not?

How many times does Paul mention Hagar by name compared to a generic description? Is he speaking about her literally or figuratively?

Think about what you know of Hagar's story so far. What key events from her story does Paul omit from his analogy?

Read 1 Corinthians 15:9. How does Paul describe himself and on what basis?

Read Romans 5:10. How are we described prior to being reconciled to God through Christ?

In his letter to the churches in Galatia, Paul is concerned, among other things, that the Christians are trusting in their works rather than in the saving work of Christ. He begins with an accusation—"you who desire to be under the law." He then goes into his discourse, deliberately fashioning a stark contrast in the minds of his readers between Sarah and Hagar. And this is where we have to be careful. Paul has a specific message he wants to get across and selects very specific elements of the story of Sarah and Hagar to make his point. He is not attempting to interpret the Genesis story or to offer any conclusions. Paul tells his readers right from the start that this is an allegory. He deliberately excludes redemptive portions of the story, and he likens each of the original individuals to something or someone else in order to make his point. As a matter of fact, one scholar suggests, "Paul's apparently arbitrary exegesis in this allegory may indicate that this was not

his choice of text . . . but that it was being used by his opponents to their own advantage."[8]

All of this is to say that to cite Galatians 4 in an attempt to define or enhance our understanding of the character or fate of Hagar or Ishmael would be a grievous error. Paul does indeed describe Ishmael's behavior as persecution in verse 29, and if Galatians 4 were the only reference concerning Hagar and Ishmael someone were to read, it is easy to see how their stories could become distorted in the mind of the reader. This is why taking a few moments to carefully study what Paul is saying, and what he is *not* saying, is so important.

PAUSE TO PONDER

Before doing this study, where would you have placed an X on the line below as it relates to Hagar's story?

tragic/sad _____ inspiring/hopeful

Where would you place an X now?

tragic/sad _____ inspiring/hopeful

As I mentioned earlier, we do not know precisely what Ishmael was doing. Some later translations added "at Isaac her son" at the end of verse 9 for clarification. While this is not included in the original Hebrew, the author's choice of words does provide the reader with an important clue. I conducted a brief word study and found that there are no less than eight different Hebrew words in the Bible that communicate some form of mocking. But the author chooses none of these. Instead, he uses the Hebrew word *tsahaq*, which is best understood as laughing or playing (the word's primary usage is "to laugh," although it can also mean jesting, making sport, mocking, or even playful affection).[9] While the author had plenty of word choices that would have made his intent more obvious, the author instead engages his reader in a word play, which is difficult to discern in the English translation.

The name Isaac in Hebrew is *Yitshaq* and, as you know, means "he laughs." Tsa-haq. Yits-haq. By using similar sounds and a play on words, the author not only succeeds in associating the two without having to spell it out, but it also helps his Hebrew audience to remember the story. This, along with Paul's attestation in Galatians 4:29 (see Supplemental Reading "Does the New Testament

Reject Hagar?"), may explain the decision of some translators to add "at Isaac her son" to the end of Genesis 21:9.

Even so, surely this would not have been the first time Ishmael had been seen interacting with, playing with, or even taunting his baby brother. There must be a reason that it was on this occasion that Sarah blew a gasket.

A Rite of Passage

> Beginning in Genesis 21:8, list the events that led up to Sarah demanding the permanent exile of Hagar and Ishmael. Be specific.

In biblical times, the weaning of a child was cause for a great celebration, as we see here when "Abraham made a great feast on the day that Isaac was weaned." The celebration commemorated a child's first transition toward independence—in this case, away from dependence upon his mother's milk. In Sarah's mind, her son was being inaugurated into the next stage of life, a rite of passage, if you will, and it was then that the son of her rival was suddenly seen as a threat.

> Let us assume for a moment that Ishmael was mocking Isaac in some way. Do you believe that Sarah's punishment fit the crime? Explain.

> What was Sarah's reason for wanting Hagar and Ishmael cast out? How does this shed light on her reaction?

························· Your Turn ·······································

Have you (or someone you deeply care about) ever experienced retaliation that seemed extreme for the offense that triggered it? If so, please answer the questions that follow.

> What "offense" did you (or your loved one) commit?

> How did the other person retaliate?

> How did you respond?

Do you wish you had responded differently? If so, how?

Looking back, could there have been something else fueling the other person's hostility? If so, describe it.

Is there someone God is bringing to your mind that you are struggling to forgive? If so, ask God to help you see the person as He sees them. In the margin, record what God reveals to you, including anything He is asking you to do.

Perhaps it was you who retaliated disproportionately or unfairly toward someone else. If you have ever experienced this, please answer the questions that follow.

What happened that offended you?

How did you retaliate?

Do you wish you had responded differently? If so, how?

Looking back, could there have been something else fueling your hostility? If so, describe it.

Is there someone from whom you need to ask forgiveness? If so, ask God to help you see yourself and the situation through His eyes. In the margin, record what God reveals to you, including anything He is asking you to do.

DAY THREE
Tossing Out Our Baby Bottles

Have you ever tried to pry a baby bottle from a child who is not ready to let go? The little darling may be sucking in nothing but air, yet he will keep milking that bottle for all it's worth. We expect that from a child, but if we are honest, there are times when we are no different.

Last week, I shared with you my story of having been laid off from my job. As I mentioned, I was actually laid off not once but three times! Now, before you raise your eyebrows, wondering if I was the problem, let me explain. It was the same job. Each time. I worked at a city-owned airport, and while my boss did not want to lay me off, I had the least seniority in our department. Due to budget cuts, he had no other choice. Over the next twenty months or so, the airport would hire me back whenever funds permitted. Each time, I hoped to get my job back only to be laid off again . . . and again . . . and again. Eventually, I accepted the airport's offer for a different position at a third less pay for a job that was a terrible fit. Meanwhile, I was in seminary, juggling bills, tuition, job searches, and class schedules. When I took one night to go away and seek clarity from the Lord, I heard Him say, "Why do you keep going back there? It was I who took you out of the airport . . . *three times*." I could almost hear the suction sound as the baby bottle fell from my face.

What? That was You?!

Apparently, I was not ready to let go. I had been working full-time since I was seventeen years old. I worked full-time all the way through college and then through graduate school (the first time). I actually liked working. It provided me with a sense of accomplishment, identity, and independence. *Bingo.* I had allowed my success in the workforce to convince me I could take care of myself. I had unwittingly created an idol.

I was subconsciously clinging to a false identity and false security. It is one thing to say God is my Provider; it is quite another to live it out in real life. It seemed God had decided it was time for me to quit my job, place my complete trust in Him, and enter seminary full-time. He knows when we are ready for the next stage of life, even if we do not. Although it took me a while to finally get the message and do as He asked, it actually felt good to toss out that old baby bottle.

PAUSE TO PONDER

How about you? Have you ever held on to something that God was gently trying to pry from your hands? Describe the situation, including what you could lose and what you could gain. *What did you learn from your experience?*

It is one thing to say God is my Provider; it is quite another to live it out in real life.

To Share and Share Alike

Read Genesis 21:8–14 (verses 8–13 are a review). List every action each of the following individuals take.

> Abraham
>
> Ishmael
>
> Sarah
>
> God
>
> Hagar

How does Sarah refer to Hagar and how many times?

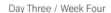 Contrast Sarah's attitude toward Hagar at this time compared to sixteen or seventeen years earlier, as we studied in Genesis 16. Has anything changed? Explain.

Answer the following questions based on what you just read in Genesis 21:8–14.

What is underlying Sarah's hostility?

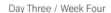 What evidence of generational conflict is at play?

One scholar writes, "It is likely that Ishmael has a legal right of inheritance. . . . [T]hat is why Sarah goes to such lengths to get rid of him. We also know, on the other hand, that people in the positions of Hagar and Ishmael were not considered fully free. . . . [T]hose in that position may be given freedom in exchange for forfeiting their property rights. That appears to be what is going on in our story: Sarah wants Hagar and Ishmael to be set free, and in return they are to disavow any claim they might have on Abraham's estate."[10] Another writes, "In that culture it was reprehensible to send Ishmael away. When a surrogate wife had borne a son to one's husband, that mother and child could not be dismissed even if the first wife subsequently gave birth to a son."[11]

In Old Testament times and even in many Middle Eastern cultures to this day, family inheritance was of extreme importance. Typically, the firstborn son could expect to receive a larger inheritance (2 Chron. 21:3), a special blessing (Gen. 27), and a place of honor (Gen. 43:33). Furthermore, "Ancient Near Eastern custom allotted a double portion of the inheritance to the firstborn."[12]

> Read Deuteronomy 21:15–17. While God never condones the practice of taking more than one wife—surrogate or otherwise—what does this regulation reveal about God's heart?

> How does this passage give you a greater appreciation of God as Protector?

Although Hagar had only been a temporary surrogate wife to Abraham, her son would have likely been recognized by everyone in the camp as a permanent, legitimate heir for the past sixteen or more years. Sarah knew this all too well.

You Meant It for Evil, but God Meant It for Good

> What was Abraham's reaction to Sarah's demands, according to Genesis 21:11?

The word commonly translated "displeasing" or "distressed" in Genesis 21:11–12 comes from the Hebrew word *raa*. It is quite a severe word that is best understood as "to be evil" (as in appearing to be evil in the person's eyes). Scripture reveals that Abraham is not only reluctant to comply with Sarah's demands, but in his eyes, to do what she asked would be evil. That's quite a strong conviction.

> Who is Abraham distressed about, according to verse 11?

> Who is not mentioned?

What might this suggest about Abraham's relationship to Hagar?

Whose voice did Abraham ultimately listen to?

Whose decision, then, was it to cast out Hagar and Ishmael?

Do you find this surprising? Upsetting? Confusing? Share your thoughts.

Even After All This Time . . . No One Knows My Name

We just read in Deuteronomy 21 that God is greatly concerned for the protection of mothers and children in Hagar and Ishmael's position. And yet, God sends Hagar and Ishmael away. Let's see if we can discover why.

How does God refer to Hagar when speaking about her to Abraham? How many times does He describe her in this manner?

Why do you suppose God uses this term when speaking to Abraham about Hagar?

Hagar is the object of discussion between Abraham and Sarah, yet again, just as we read in Genesis 16, not once is she referred to by name. Except perhaps by her son, Hagar still remains unnamed, unknown, and unloved. Even after all these years, in the eyes of Abraham and Sarah, Hagar is no more than a nameless, voiceless slave woman. As a matter of fact, we have not heard Hagar's voice since she ran away into the desert sixteen or seventeen years ago. When God likewise refers to Hagar as Abraham's "slave woman," He is simply acknowledging Hagar's standing in Abraham's eyes and perhaps in the eyes of the entire community as well—but not in His eyes. Oh no, in God's eyes, she is so much more. He sees beyond what man sees; God sees Behind the Seen.

An Identity Crisis

List everything Hagar and Ishmael stood to lose.

The situation looks quite bleak. Traditionally, custom dictated that at least Ishmael, as Abraham's son, should be provided for (as a slave, Hagar had no rights). By being sent away, Ishmael lost both his father and his inheritance. But I suspect he may have suffered the loss of something far more painful: his sense of identity and self-worth. For at least thirteen years, Ishmael had been raised to believe he was God's promised child to Abraham. This is further supported by the fact that both Abraham and Sarah expressed complete shock when the Lord announced they would soon give birth to a son. Following Isaac's birth and for two to three years afterward, where Ishmael and Hagar sensed they fit within Abraham's household is anyone's guess. Then, suddenly, they are cast out altogether. Expelled from the familiarity and protection of the community. No need for any more second-guessing. The verdict is in: they have outstayed their welcome.

God, what are you doing?

Try stepping into their sandals for a moment. How do you suppose Abraham's refusal to defend Hagar and Ishmael, though it was in accordance with God's will, was felt:

by Hagar?

by Ishmael?

God's Sovereign Plan

"But God said to Abraham . . . 'Do as she tells you'" (Gen. 21:12).

This is now the second time we see Sarah reacting harshly to what she sees as a display of disrespect. Perhaps she is overreacting, or perhaps she has endured it for so long that one day, bam! She just snaps . . . *and yet, God goes along with it?* Did we miss something? If we are tempted to question God's good judgment or character, then it is a sure bet we have missed something. What's going on here? When Sarah virtually commands Abraham to sleep with Hagar, God is silent. When Sarah orders Abraham to toss the woman and her son out into the wilderness, God speaks up—and seems keen on the idea. *Really?*

> Rather than stripping away our free will, God is often willing to work through our faults and failures to fulfill His wonderful purposes.

Yet the more I study God's interaction with His people, the more I fall in love with Him. Rather than stripping away our free will, God is often willing to work through our faults and failures to fulfill His wonderful purposes. This is perhaps one of the most beautiful demonstrations of His incredible patience and mercy. While Sarah's actions are motivated by jealousy for an earthly inheritance, God, who looks down from the heights of heaven, sees things on a far grander scale: He has eternity on His mind.

God has a plan for Isaac: to begin the lineage through which God will ultimately deliver the Savior of the world. And God also has a plan for Ishmael: to bless him and make him into a great nation (Gen. 17:20). Even though Ishmael is not the son God promised, God nonetheless kept His promise to Abraham to bless his offspring, including his beloved son Ishmael. The future of each brother has nothing to do with any inherent differences in their worth; it is the sovereign plan of God. The only decision remaining is how each will respond to God's plan.

It is the same with Sarah and Hagar. God has one plan for Sarah: to display His power by orchestrating a miracle birth, which serves as a foreshadowing for an even greater miraculous birth still to come. God also has a plan for Hagar, which we are slowly uncovering. The future of each woman has nothing to do with any inherent differences in their worth; they are the sovereign plans of God. Once again: the only decision remaining is how each will respond to God's plan.

·····················Your Turn·····················

How about you? Have you reached the point where you have embraced God's plan for your life, or is something holding you back? Is there a "baby bottle" you are still clinging to? If so, how might it be hindering your walk with God?

No matter where you are, take a few moments and ask God to help you see yourself as He sees you. Write a prayer in response to what He reveals, perhaps asking Him for the courage to embrace His plan for you or to take the next step as He reveals it to you.

DAY FOUR
Tears Falling in the Desert

A Place for Everything and Everything in Its Place

Earlier this week, I made a promise that we would explore why the events in Genesis 18–20 are placed where they are. The story flow can come across as somewhat choppy. When we come across passages that seem out of order, it is good to remind ourselves that nothing in Scripture is ever random or out of place. In Day One of this week's lesson, we looked at the connection between Genesis 20 and 21 and came face-to-face with the realization that it was God who allowed Hagar to conceive Ishmael, despite the misguided motives of Abraham and Sarah. Now let's see if we can discern why chapters 18 and 19 are placed where they are.

In Genesis 18, we were given a bird's-eye view as Abraham welcomed the Lord and His guests by serving them an elaborate meal. Forget the leftover cheese and crackers; only fresh baked bread and tender veal steaks would do. At some point during the meal, perhaps while they were reclining over a cup of camel's milk, the Lord announced to the near century-old Abraham that Sarah would soon give birth to a son. I can just picture milk squirting from Abraham's nose. Then, before Abraham could straighten his tunic, his guests suddenly stood up to leave.

Abraham, being a gracious host, "went with them to set them on their way," and he could never have guessed what would happen next. "Then the men set out from there, and they looked down toward Sodom" (Gen. 18:16).

Read Genesis 18:23 and 19:29 in the margin and then answer the questions that follow.

Think back over your previous reading of Genesis 18. Do you recall Abraham ever directly asking the Lord to spare his nephew Lot?

What might the author be trying to convey by telling us that God rescued Lot because he "remembered Abraham"?

> "You have taken account of my wanderings; Put my tears in Your bottle."
> —Psalm 56:8 NASB

> "Will you indeed sweep away the righteous with the wicked?" and "God remembered Abraham and sent Lot out of the midst of the overthrow when he overthrew the cities in which Lot had lived."
> —Genesis 18:23, 19:29

PAUSE TO PONDER

Have you experienced a time when God answered an unspoken
prayer that you did not think to ask or were too afraid to hope for?

If so, what effect did it have on your relationship with God?

If not, ask God if there may be something He did
for you that you have either forgotten or did not
recognize at the time. Write what He reveals to you.

Reread Genesis 17:18 and 17:20.

Why might the author have placed the passage of God rescuing Lot between
Genesis 17, where Abraham asks for God's blessing on Ishmael, and Genesis 21,
where Hagar and Ishmael are cast out?

In light of Abraham's love and concern for Ishmael, what might Abraham's
decision to send Hagar and Ishmael away reveal about Abraham's faith in God?

Feast or Famine

Reread Genesis 21:8 and 14. Describe the responsibilities, if any, each of the
following individuals take, according to verse 14.

Abraham

Hagar

Ishmael

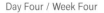

Although Abraham was very wealthy, he sent Hagar and Ishmael away with nothing except the amount of bread and water Hagar could carry on her shoulders. Yesterday, he held a great feast for his son Isaac; today, he has nothing to offer but a loaf of bread. *Really?*

Compare and contrast the feast Abraham held for Isaac and the meager supply of bread and water he gave to Hagar. What did the feast commemorate for Isaac? How might this parallel Ishmael's situation?

Scripture leaves us with no doubt that Abraham deeply loved his son Ishmael (remember Genesis 17:18?). Not only that, but he was greatly distressed at the thought of having to send him away. Although Ishmael was well on his way to becoming a man, to Abraham, he would always be his child. So when we read that he sent them away with no animals to ride and barely enough provisions to survive more than a few days, from Abraham's point of view, he is being asked to send his son to his death . . . or to surrender him into God's hands.

Nowhere to Run

Compare the events in Genesis 16:6–7 with Hagar's situation in Genesis 21:14 by completing the chart.

	Genesis 16:6–7	Genesis 21:14
Where is she?		
How did she get there?		
Where is she going?		
What do you suppose was her emotional state?		

Ponder the chart you just completed. What conclusions can you draw?

The word "wandered" in Hebrew stems from the word *taah*, meaning "to err," and has the idea of staggering or going astray.

When Hagar ran into the wilderness barefoot and pregnant, she was a naive slave girl trusting in her own independence. Had God not intervened, her self-reliance would likely have gotten her killed. Roughly sixteen years later, she is granted her freedom and the chance at a new life, but instead of heading back to Egypt or coming up with a new plan, she wanders aimlessly in the desert with barely enough food and water to keep herself alive, much less her teenaged son.

And then there is Ishmael who, for years, had basked in the pampered love and protection and, until recently, undivided attention and affection of his father. Then suddenly the privileged position is yanked right out from under his feet. Based on the flow of the text, perhaps Hagar and Ishmael never saw it coming. Nevertheless, whether there were warning signs or they were taken completely by surprise, let's imagine how this situation might have played out if God had *not* intervened by persuading Abraham to let them go.

We already know what Sarah thinks of them, "that slave woman" and that "son of the slave woman." Now just picture Abraham trying to introduce his sons—"This is my son Isaac, the miracle child from God . . . and . . . this is my other son." Or how about Hagar? Imagine how she would have felt overhearing people whispering as Ishmael walked by: "He only *thought* he was God's promise child. . . ." No matter which way you slice it, life would have been miserable for both of them. Perhaps it really was God's mercy that sent them away.

Still, hasn't poor Hagar endured enough? Used. Abused. Rejected . . . now abandoned? *God, do you see me?*

Teardrops in the Sand

Read Genesis 21:15–16. Picture the scene in your mind. Describe the desperation of the situation in your own words.

God, do you see me?

Oh yes, dear one. He sees you. Perhaps it was His love and mercy that led Him to cast you out. Maybe you are in this place at this very moment precisely because God has positioned you right where He wants you: in the wilderness. The place where battle-worn knees come crashing to the ground as a cloud of dust and darkness tries to swallow you forever, but God looks down from heaven with love in His eyes, watching the burning sand greedily devour your tears . . . listening, waiting for the moment when "she lifted up her voice and wept."

Lost. Broken. Her son is dying. She has run out of water and run out of hope. Is it any wonder Hagar is weeping? Yet it is right there, in the wilderness

> "There is no pit so deep that God's love is not deeper still."
> —Corrie ten Boom, Holocaust survivor

of heartbreak and brokenness, where her tears are finally liberated, echoing into the heavens, "Let me not look on the death of the child."

PAUSE TO PONDER

Have you ever had to face the loss of a
loved one? If so, how can you relate to Hagar?

Of all the people and events recorded in Scripture up to this point, this is the first time we encounter someone who wept.[13] And what has brought her to the point of tears? Her past? Loneliness? Rejection? No. None of these. "Let me not look on the death of the child." Hagar is weeping because she is facing the very real possibility of having to watch her son die. As a matter of fact, Hagar is the first person in all of Scripture[14] to come face-to-face with death threatening to take the life of her one and only child.

"Fear Not"

Read Genesis 21:17-19.

Try to imagine for a moment what this must have been like for Ishmael. While we know from Scripture that both Abraham and Hagar loved Ishmael, from his perspective, in his most desperate hour, he has been rejected by his father and abandoned by his mother.

God, do you see me?

Oh yes, dear one. He sees you. Perhaps it was His love and mercy that led Him to cast you out. Maybe you are in this place at this very moment precisely because God has positioned you right where He wants you: in the wilderness. The place where battle-worn knees come crashing to the ground as a cloud of dust and darkness tries to swallow you forever, but God looks down from heaven with love in His eyes, watching the burning sand greedily devour your tears . . . and He hears your voice right where you are.

How is Ishmael's name represented in the text? (For a hint, reread Genesis 16:11).

"The eyes of the LORD are toward the righteous and his ears toward their cry.

—Psalm 34:15

"The angel of the LORD encamps around those who fear him, and delivers them." —Psalm 34:7

Contrast Hagar's divine encounter in Genesis 21:15–19 with her first encounter in Genesis 16:8–11. In the margin, list every similarity and every difference you notice. What insights can you discover?

Read Psalm 34:7 in the margin. How does this verse shed light on how God sees Hagar?

"Fear not." Consider the magnitude of those two little words when spoken by God Almighty, the Holy One whom we should all fear. For God to comfort Hagar with these words speaks volumes about His relationship to her. The expression "fear not" (or "do not fear" or "do not be afraid") is recorded merely seven times in the book of Genesis and occurs in less than one hundred verses in the entire Bible.[15]

Look up at least five of the passages in the chart below; then, for each one, complete the chart as follows.

In the second column, state who is giving the message.

In the third column, write the name of (or describe) the person who is being spoken to.

In the fourth column, briefly describe the persons being spoken to. Who are they? What do you know or what have you heard about them? (If they are not familiar to you, it's okay to leave the space blank.)

Finally, in the last column, summarize the primary purpose of the message.

I completed the first one to get you started.

Reference	Who is speaking?	Who is being spoken to?	Describe the recipient(s).	What is the purpose of the message?
Genesis 15:1	The Lord	Abraham	Father of Faith	Encouragement; announce a reward
Genesis 21:17				
Genesis 26:17, 23–24				

Genesis 46:2–3				
Numbers 21:34				
Joshua 8:1				
Judges 6:23–24				
Daniel 10:12				
Matthew 1:20				
Luke 1:26–31				
Luke 1:11–13				
Luke 2:8–11				
Revelation 1:9, 17–18				

What common themes do you notice in the messages?

Although we have only looked at a sample of "fear not" references in the Bible,[16] if you were to conduct an exhaustive study, you would find that the vast majority are spoken by either God Himself or His messenger, such as an angel or prophet, in order to comfort, encourage, or strengthen His servants.

After Abraham (Gen. 15:1), Hagar is the very next person in the Bible whom God visits and comforts with the words "fear not." From there, we read about Isaac, Jacob, Moses . . . the Twelve, Mary, Zechariah . . . and the list of His servants goes on and on. Hagar is in quite good company, wouldn't you say?

Trusting in God's Protection

Compare how God addresses Hagar in Genesis 16 compared to Genesis 21.

What changed?

What significance might this have?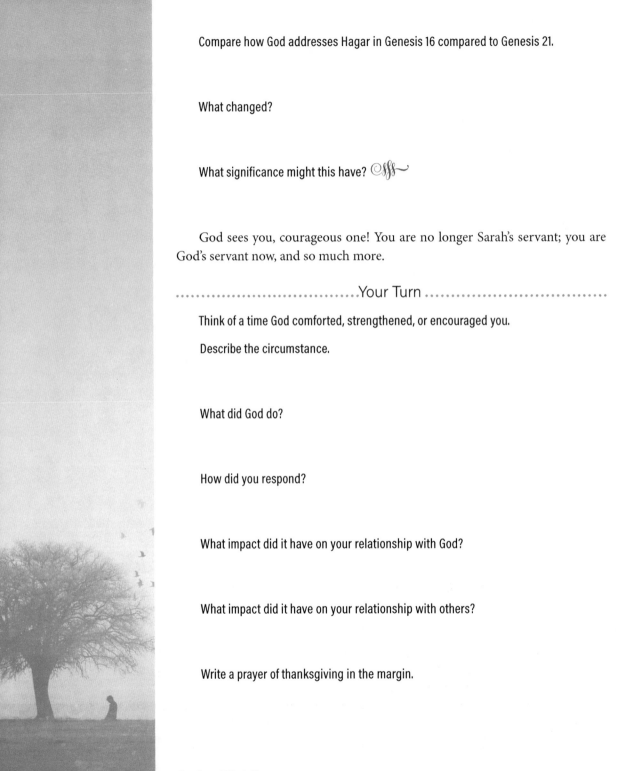

God sees you, courageous one! You are no longer Sarah's servant; you are God's servant now, and so much more.

························Your Turn ·······························

Think of a time God comforted, strengthened, or encouraged you.

Describe the circumstance.

What did God do?

How did you respond?

What impact did it have on your relationship with God?

What impact did it have on your relationship with others?

Write a prayer of thanksgiving in the margin.

DAY FIVE
Embracing God's Call

"She lifted up her voice and wept" (Gen. 21:16).

Fear not, child, for El Roi *is the God who sees you. He is rich in love and mercy; He sees your sorrow and hears your cry. You are not alone.*

If only Hagar could see herself through His eyes. The God who promised her, "I will surely multiply your offspring so that they cannot be numbered for multitude" (Gen. 16:10) has not changed and cannot fail. He still sits on the throne in heaven's throne room. But before Hagar could stand and embrace her call, she had to fall to her knees, surrender her idol of self-reliance, and come face-to-face with her complete and utter dependence on God. The moment her cry passed over heaven's threshold, God answered, "What troubles you, Hagar?"

Guardian Angels

Compare Genesis 19:15–16 with 21:18–19 and then answer the questions that follow.

Genesis 19:15–16:

What was Lot asked to do?

How did Lot respond?

What did God's angels do? Be specific.

Genesis 21:18–19:

What was Hagar asked to do? Be specific.

What did God do for Hagar?

> Before we can stand and embrace our call, we must fall to our knees, surrender our idols of self-reliance, and come face-to-face with our complete and utter dependence on God.

> "Up! Lift up the boy, and hold him fast with your hand, for I will make him into a great nation."
> —Genesis 21:18

How did Hagar respond?

Whose actions closely parallel each other in these two passages? Do you find this interesting? Inspiring? Share your thoughts in the margin.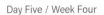

Had the events in Genesis 18 and 19 not been recorded for us and placed precisely where they were, we may never have fully appreciated the magnitude of the task God ordained for Hagar to fulfill. Just as God, in His mercy, sent angels to rescue Abraham's beloved nephew Lot, He appointed Hagar to rescue the beloved Ishmael.

But God did not stop there.

The phrase translated "hold fast" (or simply "hold" in some translations) is derived from the Hebrew word *chazaq*, which means "grow strong" or "to strengthen." In effect, while God Almighty needs no one or nothing, in His grace, He invites Hagar to trust Him as He fulfills His plan for Ishmael: as Hagar helps Ishmael to grow strong, God will keep His promise to make him into a great nation. I cannot think of any purpose in life more significant than to trust God and be invited to join Him in His holy work, can you?

Once I Was Blind, Now I See

"Then God opened her eyes" (Gen. 21:19).

This is the first occurrence we read in Scripture where God opens a person's eyes.[17] This is remarkable because in the Bible, physical blindness is often used as an analogy for spiritual blindness[18]—an inability to recognize the One True God and the honor due Him. Yet when Hagar's cry reached heaven, God was ready to open her eyes and display His deliverance.

Read Luke 18:35–43. According to Jesus, what was needed for the man to be healed of his blindness?

Keeping Luke 18:35–43 in mind, compare and contrast Hagar's situation in Genesis 21:14–19 before and after God "opened her eyes" by answering the following questions.

Describe Hagar's situation before God spoke to Hagar and opened her eyes.

Describe Hagar's situation after God spoke to Hagar and opened her eyes.

While it is God who opened her eyes, what role may Hagar's faith have had?

"Though the Lord give you the bread of adversity and the water of affliction, yet your Teacher will not hide himself anymore, but your eyes shall see your Teacher. And your ears shall hear a word behind you, saying, 'This is the way, walk in it,' when you turn to the right or when you turn to the left" (Isa. 30:20–21).

> Yes, Lord, be our Teacher;
>> be our guide.
> Lead us to your cleansing waters
>> as we walk humbly by your side.

A Desert Dwelling

Read Genesis 21:20-21.

Where did Hagar and Ishmael live, according to Genesis 21:21?

Did God command them to live elsewhere? Do you think this is relevant? Why or why not?

Look up at least two of the passages listed. Record what you learn about the place Hagar and Ishmael lived.

Numbers 10:11-12; 12:16; and 13:3, 26

Deuteronomy 33:1-2

1 Samuel 23:13, 26; 25:1 (Be careful not to overlook the last portion of 1 Samuel 25:1.)

Habakkuk 3:3-4

We know that God is omnipresent, meaning He is present everywhere at the same time; however, in Old Testament times, God chose specific geographical locations where He would interact with His people and display His glory.[19] Thomas Dozeman, Professor of Old Testament at United Theological Seminary, writes, "Paran has theological as well as geographical significance already in Israel's earliest traditions of theophany [visible manifestations of God], as one designation of God's desert home."[20]

Paran, which means beauty[21] or fruitful,[22] is a wilderness located in the east central region of the Sinai Peninsula. It is the place where the Israelites camped on their way to the Promised Land during the Exodus. It is also the place where King David sought refuge, and according to the books of Deuteronomy and Habakkuk, Paran is where the glory of God bursts forth in dazzling splendor.

. . . and it is also the place where God sent Hagar and Ishmael to live.

The Cost of Freedom

What did Hagar gain as a result of being cast out of Abraham's camp? Check all that apply and add any others you can think of.

What did Hagar gain?	Check if yes
Riches	☐
Encounter with the Living God	☐
A husband	☐
Her freedom	☐
Partner with God to raise her son	☐
Other: _____	☐
Other: _____	☐

Hagar may have lost temporary comfort and security, but she gained so much more. She was no longer a slave, and with God's help, she took her son by the hand and watched him grow into a strong young man. Stepping up to the challenge normally reserved for the father, Hagar secured a wife for her son. Some commentators bemoan Hagar's choice of an Egyptian wife. Considering Hagar and Ishmael's banishment from Abraham's tribe, and Egypt likely being the only other place that may have felt familiar, Hagar's choice may not be so surprising. Whatever the reason, even in this regard, Ishmael is in good company.

Read Numbers 12:1-9 and then answer the following questions.

What nationality is Moses's wife?

148

Day Five / Week Four

Who disapproves?

Who comes to Moses's defense?

Cush is a region of the upper Nile, south of Egypt, and it roughly corresponds to modern-day Ethiopia. While God would later institute regulations for the Israelites against marrying foreigners for His own purposes, there was no such prohibition during the lives of Hagar and Ishmael and, later, Moses. As a matter of fact, we recently studied in Genesis 17 (Week Three) how God's covenant provided for the inclusion of foreigners.

I AM with You

Perhaps the best way to appreciate the immense weight of the tiny phrase "And God was with the boy" is to try to imagine the implications if Scripture had said regarding Ishmael (or anyone else for that matter), "And God was *not* with him." I don't know about you, but if I were to read those words in Scripture about anyone, anyone at all, it would make me shudder.

> Who do you know personally that has a strong walk with God? What does that look like in everyday life?

> What do you suppose most contributes to their strong relationship with God?

> If you have an opportunity, ask them what they think has most served to strengthen their relationship with God. Come back and record what you learned.

The verb in the sentence "And God *was* with the boy" is extremely important. In English, the construction of the phrase is somewhat ordinary and might not draw our attention. It could be interpreted as God was previously with the boy, is just now starting to be with the boy, or something else. Thankfully, the original Hebrew does not use a simple past tense form, but instead it uses the Hebrew

"And God was with
the boy…"
—Genesis 21:20

Trusting in God's Protection

imperfect, which can be used to communicate the beginning of something that started in the past and is continuing to occur. In other words, the phrase seems to imply that God *has been* with the boy and *continues to be* with him.

What a precious thought! And once again, we find Ishmael included in a very distinguished group. The people in the Bible of whom it says "God was with [them]" include Abraham, Noah, Isaac, Jacob, Joseph, Moses, David, John the Baptist, and Mary (the mother of Jesus), as well as numerous kings, prophets, and leaders and, of course, Jesus.

And yet, what we tend to forget about their stories is that it is often in the dark and lonely places where God meets them. Many people in the Bible of whom it says "God was with [them]" or who are described as being God's servants experienced times when they felt forgotten and abandoned. You may already be familiar with some of their stories; others you may need to look up. Let's take a look at a few.

Choose at least three of the following passages to read in your Bible. Record the name of the person experiencing the trial and briefly describe what he suffered.

	Reference	Name	What he suffered
1	Genesis 37:23–24, 28		
2	Matthew 11:2; 14:10		
3	Daniel 6:16		
4	Mark 14:66–72		
5	Job 1:14–19; 2:7		

Walking with God is never easy. He never said it would be. But we can rest in God's promise: "I will never leave you nor forsake you" (Heb. 13:5).

Next, for every row numbered one through five that you completed in the previous chart, fill out the same row numbers below (in other words, if you chose to complete rows 1, 3, and 4 above, then complete 1, 3, and 4 below). After reading the passage, record the person's name and what the Scripture says about him after his hardship.

	Reference	Name	Outcome
1	Genesis 45:4–8, 15; 50:20		
2	Matthew 11:9–11		
3	Daniel 6:21–22, 25–27		
4	Luke 24:34 (also John 21)		
5	Job 1:22; 42:10, 12–17; James 5:11		

Which person's story stood out to you the most? Why?

If you could speak to any person in the previous list, do you suppose he would tell you he had any regrets? Explain.

......................................Your Turn......................................

Because we live in a fallen world, it is inevitable that people will let us down. At the end of Day One of this week's lesson, I asked you if you had ever felt abandoned (abandonment can be physical separation, but it may also include the emotional pain of loneliness, abuse, or neglect, as we learned from Mary Slessor's story).

Think back on a time you felt lonely or abandoned. Spend some time in prayer asking God to help you see the situation from His perspective. Then complete the following sentence.

When I was _____ [approximate age(s)], I felt lonely or abandoned when _____ [describe the situation]. But God _____ _____ [describe how God revealed Himself, or protected or comforted you, or used the events for good].

If you are unable to recognize God's hand in your circumstances, spend some time this week in prayer and ask God to help you see how He intervened or is using the situation for good. Perhaps, as with Hagar, He has enabled you to take someone else by the hand and strengthen that person in his or her time of need. When you are ready, come back and complete the fill-in sentence as God enables you.

Lesson Summary

What Scripture, statement, or thought was most significant to you this week? Write it below and then reword it into a prayer of response to God in the margin.

Two worship songs that beautifully capture the heart of this week's lesson are "You Are My Hiding Place" by Selah and "You Don't Miss a Thing" by Amanda Cook.

Notes

[1] For further exploration of Mary Slessor's story, you may enjoy W. P. Livingstone's *Mary Slessor of Calabar: Heroes of the Faith* (Uhrichsville, OH: Barbour Publishing, 1986).

[2] See Romans 4:11–12.

[3] W. Smith, "Abimelech," in *Smith's Bible Dictionary* (Nashville: Thomas Nelson, 1986), Logos edition.

[4] See 1 Peter 1:20; 2 Timothy 1:8–9.

[5] See Genesis 14:14.

[6] E. D. Radmacher, R. B. Allen, and H. W. House, 1 Samuel 1:22, *The Nelson Study Bible: New King James Version* (Nashville: Thomas Nelson, 1997).

[7] M. G. Easton, "Wean," in *Easton's Bible Dictionary* (New York: Harper & Brothers, 1893), Logos edition.

[8] Nancy L. Calvert, "Abraham," in *Dictionary of Paul and His Letters*, eds. G. F. Hawthorne, R. P. Martin, and D. G. Reid (Downers Grove, IL: InterVarsity Press, 1993).

[9] The same word is used in Genesis 26:8–9. When the king sees Isaac *laughing* with his wife Rebekah, the king immediately concludes the woman must be Isaac's wife, *not* his sister, as the king had been led to believe.

[10] J. D. Currid, *A Study Commentary on Genesis*, vol. 1, *Genesis 1:1–25:18* (Darlington, England: Evangelical Press, 2003), 375.

[11] E. D. Radmacher, R. B. Allen, and H. W. House, Genesis 21:10, *The Nelson Study Bible: New King James Version* (Nashville: Thomas Nelson, 1997).

[12] C. Chambers, "Firstborn," in *The Lexham Bible Dictionary*, eds. J. D. Barry et al., (Bellingham, WA: Lexham Press, 2015) Logos edition.

[13] There is one symbolic reference to crying in Genesis 4:10, when God confronts Cain (after Cain kills his brother) by asking, "What have you done? The voice of your brother's blood is crying to me from the ground."

[14] While Adam and Eve lived through the death of their beloved son, he was neither their only child at the time nor did they endure the heart-wrenching experience of being an eyewitness to their son's suffering or death.

[15] The popular saying that there are 365 "fear not" verses in the Bible is incorrect.

[16] Here "fear not" includes occurrences of the similar phrases "do not fear" and "do not be afraid."

[17] The only prior mention in Scripture of someone's eyes being opened occurs in Genesis 3, which is entirely unlike the events in Genesis 21. In Genesis 3, Adam and Eve sinned and as a result "their eyes were opened," producing guilt, shame, and fear.

[18] See John 9:39–41; read the full chapter for context. See also Ephesians 1:18.

[19] Even here, it is understood that these manifestations are severely limited, for no human can see God as He truly is, or His glory in all of its splendor, and live.

[20] Thomas B. Dozeman, "The Wilderness and Salvation History in the Hagar Story," *Journal of Biblical Literature* 117, no. 1 (1998): 36.

[21] W. MacDonald, *Believer's Bible Commentary: Old and New Testaments*, ed. A. Farstad (Nashville: Thomas Nelson, 1995), lxi.

[22] S. Smith and J. Cornwall, *The Exhaustive Dictionary of Bible Names* (Alachua, FL: Bridge-Logos, 1998), 191.

PART III

WAITING

NOTES

SURRENDERING TO
GOD'S
PLAN

LAST WEEK, WE WERE LEFT HANGING REGARDING THE end of Hagar's story because there is a bigger picture at stake. This week, as we study God's command to Abraham to surrender the life of his son into His hands, we will discover that the same God who saw Hagar's suffering as her child lay dying is the same God who will provide a solution to an even greater need.

DAY ONE
Preparing for the Journey

"Many of the Bible's greatest themes are seen only in the sweeping landscape of the divine story; they are expressed more in vistas than in verses. To catch sight of these themes we need a different perspective, a shift in viewpoint. Rather than a microscope, we need a mountaintop." —Christopher S. Webb[1]

A Panoramic View

Scripture is rich and complex; it is both deep and wide. Sometimes we begin our day by going deep, examining details as in a lab with a microscope. Other times, it helps to step back and explore the big picture as if standing atop a mountain with a telescope. Before we dive into the beautiful details of Genesis 22, let us first step back and take in a panoramic view of the events that precede and follow the chapter.

When we last read of Hagar and Ishmael, they had been abandoned and cast out into the desert with little more than a few days' worth of bread and water. Wandering aimlessly, Hagar cried helplessly as her only child lay dying at death's door. But God was always working Behind the Seen. He opened Hagar's eyes and saved both Hagar and her son. It was there—in her desert of despair—that God reaffirmed His promises for her and her son's future. But God did so much more than that: Scripture assures us that as Ishmael grew, "God was with the boy." What a glorious picture of God's tenderness and faithfulness. Still, just when the story reaches its climax, we are left hanging. As a matter of fact, with the exception of an indirect reference in Genesis 25, Hagar is never heard from again. Let's see if we can discover why.

> Aside from God Himself, list the five primary individuals in the story we have been studying up to this point.

Very often, when a detailed account of a person's life is recorded in Scripture, the last thing we read are the facts surrounding his or her death, including his or her lineage if it was not referenced earlier.

> Read the following passages; then complete the chart by listing each person who died, along with any additional details included in the passage.

Scripture reference	Who died?	What details are mentioned?
Genesis 23:1-2, 19		
Genesis 25:1, 7-10		
Genesis 25:16-18		
Genesis 35:28-29		

The individual stories of Abraham, Sarah, Ishmael, and Isaac all come to an end . . . but wait, where is Hagar? You can search the entire Bible for the end of Hagar's story, but I will save you the trouble: it is not in there. Hagar: the first person to meet the Angel of the Lord, the first—and only[2]—person to give God a name, and the first person we read of in the Bible who suffered the agony of watching her only child lying at death's door . . . and there is no closure? No mention of her death? Did God forget her? Did the author get distracted? Is there a page missing? No . . . no . . . no. We are left hanging, but sandwiched in between the story of Hagar and Ishmael being driven into the desert and the accounts of Isaac and Ishmael "breathing their last" is the famous Genesis 22.

The Big Picture

While we will explore Genesis 22 in greater detail in the days ahead, I would like you to take some time right now to get an overview of the big picture.

Read Genesis 22:1-19 at least two times all the way through (consider reading it at least once out loud).

Center your attention on Genesis 22:1-2.

What is God's motivation for the instructions He gives to Abraham?

List everything God tells Abraham to do.

How does God describe Abraham's final destination? Be specific.

God tells Abraham to go to the land of Moriah—to a specific mountain God will later reveal to him. No one is certain of the meaning or origin of the word *Moriah*. Some Bible dictionaries "link the word to the act of seeing,"[3] such as "Seen of Jehovah"[4] or "Visible of the Lord."[5] One commentator suggests that the name is "a word-play on two verbs which both play an important part in the episode: 'to see' (Hebrew *r-'-h*) and 'to fear' (Hebrew *y-r-'*)."[6] Moriah is referenced in the Bible for the first time in this passage and appears again only one other time in the entire Bible.

Read 2 Chronicles 3:1; 5:1; and 6:1-6.

What was built at this location?

Who chose the place where God's house would be built, according to 2 Chronicles 6:6?

Roughly one thousand years before the first temple of God was constructed, God sent Abraham to that very same site. Dr. Sandra Scham, professor and expert in Middle Eastern Archeology, writes, "Today, Mount Moriah refers to the Temple Mount for Jews, Golgotha for Christians, and the Dome of the Rock for Muslims."[7] There is no other place on all the earth revered by more people than this site.

Which of the following best reflects Abraham's response to God's command in Genesis 22:2? Circle one.

He obeyed after receiving his wife's approval.

He waited for a more convenient time to travel.

He obeyed and went.

If this question sounds familiar, it is because we pondered it in Week One. The first time we learn of Abraham hearing from God is in Genesis 12:1. The last direct revelation from God to Abraham is recorded in Genesis 22.

Compare Genesis 12:1 with Genesis 22:2 and then answer the questions that follow.

What similarities can you discover?

What progressions do you notice unfolding when you compare the two passages?

How did God prepare Abraham for his second journey?

What does this reveal about God's character?

"Go from your country and your kindred and your father's house to the land that I will show you."
—Genesis 12:1

In both scenarios, Abraham had to walk by faith. Not only that, but he was asked to surrender (or separate himself from) those he loved. And while the destination was more clear in the second journey, the separation was infinitely more sorrowful.

PAUSE TO PONDER

> Try to imagine for a moment that you are
> Abraham. What thoughts or feelings may have
> surfaced upon hearing God call Isaac "your only son"?

Given that Abraham had two sons by this time, the expression "your only son" can be misunderstood. Whenever we find passages in the Bible that seem confusing or conflicting, we must ask God to help us as we examine the whole truth of Scripture. The specific Hebrew word translated "only" in Genesis 22:2 is *yahid*.

My Precious Life

The following two verses are copied from the ESV translation. I have italicized the translation of the Hebrew word "only" in both passages. Take a look.

"Deliver my soul from the sword, my *precious life* from the power of the dog!" (Ps. 22:20).

"How long, O Lord, will you look on? Rescue me from their destruction, my *precious life* from the lions!" (Ps. 35:17).

How is the word "only" used in these passages? What does the psalmist seem to be feeling?

The same word also appears in the following verses. Read at least one of these verses in your Bible. What can you discover regarding how the word "only" is used?

Jeremiah 6:26   Amos 8:10   Zechariah 12:10

The Hebrew word *yahid* occurs merely twelve times in the entire Old Testament, with three of those occurrences appearing in a single chapter—namely, Genesis 22. In the two verses you just read from the Psalms, the word is equated with one's own life, and in Psalms 25:16 and 68:6, the word refers to someone who is solitary or lonely. In the remaining eight of the twelve occurrences, the word refers to the welfare of an only son or child, particularly parental anguish over the death of an only son.[8] Abraham had already lost his son Ishmael when God sent him away,

"We walk by faith, not by sight," and "Faith is the assurance of things hoped for, the conviction of things not seen."
—2 Corinthians 5:7 and Hebrews 11:1

so Abraham would naturally feel as if Isaac were an only son. Not only that, Isaac is the child promised to Abraham by God Himself, making the idea of sacrificing him that much more agonizing.

A SIGN

The use of the Hebrew word *ya-hid* implies even more than what we have already discovered.

Read John 3:16 and Hebrews 11:17. What similarities can you discover in these two verses?

The same Greek word *monogene*, translated "only" (some translations, "only begotten") is used in both passages. One commentator explains, "monogenē comes from monos ["alone, only"] and genē ("kind"), so the term means 'unique.' This means that Jesus was the unique Son of God. [Likewise, in Hebrews] . . . the term refers to Isaac's special status, not his birth or birth order."[9]

Isaac is unique as the promised child of God, conceived by divine intervention. When we read of God referring to Isaac as Abraham's only son, we need to recognize this is not a dismissal of Ishmael (we just read in Genesis 21 that "God was with the boy"), but rather it is intended to serve as a sign, pointing to Jesus Christ, who would be born roughly two thousand years later by the singular most unique and miraculous human conception in the history of the world: a virgin birth.

Your Turn

Sometimes God asks us to surrender tangible things, such as people or possessions, but there are other times when He asks us to surrender things that are unseen, such as our hopes, ideas, or dreams. There are instances when, as with God's instructions to Abraham, we know exactly what God wants. Then there are those moments when God's voice is more subtle as He gently leads us to a place of surrender.

Think back on a time when God asked you to surrender something to Him.

What was your initial response?

Was there an obstacle in your way? (An obstacle can be external, but it may also be internal, such as fear or rebellion.)

If there was an obstacle, how did you respond to it?

What did you learn about yourself or God through this experience?

When it comes to having a relationship with God, why is surrender so important?

DAY TWO
Facing Your Mountain

Recently, some dear friends brought home a bouncing white puppy named Rudy. When my friends mentioned they would be departing for a trip a few weeks later, I volunteered to take care of Rudy for the weekend. I like dogs, I love going for afternoon walks, and although it had been a few years since I had a pet, I had owned dogs most of my adult life. Besides, Rudy was five pounds; how much trouble could he be? It was not like I was completely in the dark. I expected a tiny piddle here and there, and I knew I would not get much writing done that weekend.

Even so, there were a few surprises. By the end of day two, his razor-sharp puppy teeth left my hands looking like they had been through a paper shredder. But that is not all. Five pounds did not sound like much . . . until the first time I took the little rascal for a walk. I look forward to my walks; they are a time of worship for me. Typically, I listen to praise music on my iPod while talking with God and admiring the beauty of His creation. What a difference five feisty pounds makes! I felt as if a mini rocket strapped to a dumbbell had been tethered to my wrist. Three times I nearly fell when Rudy darted between my feet, tangling his leash around my ankles.

For a full thirty minutes, my arm was jerked every which way as Rudy bounded after squirrels, fluttering leaves, or anything else that caught his eye. Never once did I look up and admire God's creation; instead, I was either focused on my feet as I tried to avoid stepping on the little guy, or I was looking in whichever new direction Rudy was pulling me. To top it off, although my music was playing and my earbuds were firmly in place, I do not think I consciously heard one song. When Rudy paused to dive into and roll around in a lush bed of clover, I paused as well, thinking it was nothing at all like the worshipful walks I was used to. I never imagined that something so small and innocent could be such a distraction!

The Mountain of Testing

As we learned in Day One of this week's lesson, God had decided to put Abraham's faith to the test. God is omniscient, which means He knows everything. It was Abraham who needed to discover whether there was anything that stood in the way of his devotion to God. Not all idols are obvious. Some can appear completely innocent, but if we are not careful, anything we allow to come between us and God will eventually leave us tangled, disoriented, exhausted, and unable to hear His voice. The reality is that God will have only one of two places in our lives: first place or no place.

> God will have only one of two places in our lives: first place or no place.

What comes to mind when you think of idolatry? How would you describe it?

Read Ephesians 5:5 and Colossians 3:5.

How does Scripture describe idolatry, according to these verses?

How does it compare with your definition?

> Not all idols are physical. Ideas, hopes, and dreams can become idols as well.

Generally speaking, idolatry is "the worship of something created as opposed to the worship of the Creator Himself,"[10] or simply, "anything receiving worship other than the one true God."[11] Therefore, idolatry not only includes the worship of physical things, such as people (either ourselves or others), other creatures, or possessions, but ideas, hopes, and dreams can become idols as well.

Idols can also be temporary. The desire for new kitchen cabinets, the longing for intimacy, the dream to have a child, a ministry you are passionate about, or success at work or school—any one of these can become an idol if, for even a moment, we give them first place in our hearts.

PAUSE TO PONDER

List some potential idols that are
competing for your attention right now.

Have you or someone you know ever suffered under the
weight of an idol? Describe the situation and the effect it had.

What are some ways idols can wreak havoc in
people's lives? List as many as you can think of.

In Genesis 22:2, in addition to referring to Isaac as Abraham's "only son," how else does God describe him?

This is the first time the word *love* appears in the Bible. God Himself describes Isaac as Abraham's only son "whom you love," revealing to Abraham that God knew full well how much Isaac meant to him. While this is the first occurrence of the word love, this does not suggest that this is the first time love entered human history. There are many relationships where love, often between parent and child, is clearly understood and assumed in the Bible. Examples include Adam and Eve grieving over the death of their son, Abraham pleading with God for Ishmael's future, and Hagar being tormented by the impending death of her only child. All of these reveal that love was very much present in the lives of people. However, because the first usage of a key word in Scripture often sets its tone, it is worth our while to examine why the word love is first included here.

What comes to mind when you think of love? How would you define it?

What are some other ways people might define love? List as many as you can think of.

Read John 3:16 and Romans 5:8 and then answer the questions that follow.

How does Scripture present love?

How does it compare with your definition?

How does it compare with the world's definition?

The Mountain of Temptation

Reread Genesis 22:4–8. How many days did Abraham walk before his destination came into view?

Imagine yourself in Abraham's position. What temptations may he have faced along the way?

Genesis 22:5 describes Isaac as a boy (some translations say *lad*), but this can be misleading. The Hebrew word for boy (or lad) in this verse is *naar*, which is commonly translated "young man" or "servant." The same word is used to describe Abraham's young men (or servants) in verses 3 and 5. Because Isaac was tasked with hauling enough wood up the side of a mountain to set ablaze a sizable sacrifice, many scholars estimate Isaac was at least a teenager—or even in his twenties or thirties—by this time. This would suggest that at least ten to as many as thirty years had passed since God sent Hagar and Ishmael away. The author likewise alludes to this when he writes, "And Abraham sojourned *many days* in the land of the Philistines" (Gen. 21:34; emphasis mine).

Glance back at Genesis 21:10–11. What was Abraham's initial reaction to the idea of losing his son Ishmael?

Reread Genesis 22:2–3. Compare and contrast Abraham's response in this passage with that in Genesis 21:10–11.

〜 What are some possible reasons that may account for the difference in how Abraham responded in each case?

"We Will Worship"

Just as the first occurrences of the words *only* and *love* are found in Genesis 22, the word *worship* also appears in the Bible for the first time in this chapter. While the concept of worship is portrayed in Scripture prior to this passage (Gen. 12:7–8; also Gen. 4:4 and 8:20), this is the first time the word worship is recorded in the Bible. And what do we discover? Not only is the word directly linked to sacrifice, but it is a sacrifice of that which is most precious to the worshiper.

What comes to mind when you hear the word *worship*? How would you describe it?

What are some other ways people might define worship? List as many as you can think of.

Read Romans 12:1 in your Bible and Exodus 20:3 and 20:5a in the margin. How is worship represented in these passages?

What new insights did you gain? How does your definition of worship compare with Scripture?

> "You shall have no other gods before me.... You shall not bow down to them or serve them, for I the LORD your God am a jealous God."
> —Exodus 20:3, 5a

One of the many wonderful treasures of having access to God's written Word is the opportunity for us to regularly reassess our view of God, ourselves, and the world around us.

Write what Abraham said to his servants in Genesis 22:5.

What do Abraham's words reveal about his faith?

Read Hebrews 11:17–19 and compare it with Genesis 22:5. What do these verses reveal about Abraham's faith?

The phrase, "We will come again [or return] to you," in the original Hebrew implies a very strong determination: we *will* come again. This is further emphasized by the repeated use of "and"[12] in Abraham's dialogue with his servants: "[We] will go . . . *and* worship *and* come again to you" (Gen. 22:5; emphasis mine).

Talk about faith!

The Mountain of Sorrow

Center your attention on Genesis 22:5–6; then answer the following questions.

Who was left behind and who set out to climb the mountain?

Describe the objects that the father and son each carried up the mountain.

What other burdens might each of them have been carrying?

Genesis 22:5 makes it clear that only Abraham and Isaac would be journeying onward, yet at the end of verse 6, the author points out that "they went both of them together."

What might the author be trying to convey by adding this comment?

In Genesis 22:7, Isaac speaks for the first time.

What does he say?

Glance back at verse 6. What object does Isaac not mention?

Imagine the scene from Isaac's point of view. Abraham was very wealthy, having many flocks and herds of all kinds of animals. For three days, they have been hauling a mass of wood along rugged terrain for a sacrifice. Abraham remembered the fire and the knife as well, but he left behind an entire sheep pen full of lambs. Surely it would have been easier to pick up some timber during their three-day hike rather than a lonely, wandering lamb.

How does Abraham answer Isaac's question in Genesis 22:8? Write Abraham's response below.

What does Abraham's response reveal about his faith?

After Abraham answers his son, the author repeats the same phrase: "They went both of them together." Once again, what might the author be trying to convey here?

In this passage, we are presented with the beautiful reminder that all along the way, the father and son walked in harmony with one another. And while Isaac carried the wood, his father carried a grave burden as well: the weapon of destruction.

....................................Your Turn ....

Mountains come in all shapes and sizes. Throughout our lives, you and I will face many mountains: some big, some small.

What kind of mountain are you facing right now? A test of faith? A temptation? A sorrow? An unknown? Describe the situation.

What would it look like for you to climb your mountain "in harmony" with God?

DAY THREE
Climbing the Mountain Together

In Week One, we discovered that we can learn a lot by studying the structure of a Biblical text. A literary pattern called chiastic structure is one method commonly found in Scripture. In a chiastic structure (or chiasm or chiasmus), the author lays out a sequence of words, concepts, or events and then presents an identical or similar sequence in reverse order.[14]

The goal is to draw the reader's attention to the middle: to the location within the passage where the inverted sequences intersect one another. It is at this point of intersection that we discover what the author wants to emphasize. To help readers visualize a chiastic pattern, biblical scholars typically use pairs of letters to identify parallel words, phrases, or concepts (A is parallel to A', B is parallel to B', and so on), as we studied in Week One.

Walking by Faith

Read Genesis 22:4-13, which is included below. This passage forms a chiastic structure, which I have outlined following the text. As you read the passage, try to identify parallel words and phrases. When you are finished, fill in the blanks on the outline. Keep in mind that when outlining a chiasm, it is not necessary to record every word in the text, but rather to identify parallel words, phrases, or concepts. I filled in a few to get you started.

"On the third day Abraham lifted up his eyes and saw the place from afar. Then Abraham said to his young men, "Stay here with the donkey; I and the boy will go over there and worship and come again to you." And Abraham took the wood of the burnt offering and laid it on Isaac his son. And he took in his hand the fire and the knife. So they went both of them together. And Isaac said to his father Abraham, "My father!" And he said, "Here I am, my son." He said, "Behold, the fire and the wood, but where is the lamb for a burnt offering?" Abraham said, "God will provide for himself the lamb for a burnt offering, my son." So they went both of them together.
When they came to the place of which God had told him, Abraham built the altar there and laid the wood in order and bound Isaac his son and laid him on the altar, on top of the wood. Then Abraham reached out his hand and took the knife to slaughter his son. But the

"God never tells us to give up things just for the sake of giving them up, but He tells us to give them up for the sake of the only thing worth having, namely, life with Himself."

—Oswald Chambers[13]

Angel of the LORD called to him from heaven and said, "Abraham, Abraham!" And he said, "Here I am." He said, "Do not lay your hand on the boy or do anything to him, for now I know that you fear God, seeing you have not withheld your son, your only son, from me." And Abraham lifted up his eyes and looked, and behold, behind him was a ram, caught in a thicket by his horns. And Abraham went and took the ram and offered it up as a burnt offering instead of his son."

A   Abraham *lifted up his eyes*

   B   Abraham *spoke*

      C   I and the boy will go over there

           AND _____ and come again

           AND Abraham took the _____ of the burnt offering

           AND laid it on _____

           AND took in his _____ the fire

           AND the _____

         D   So they went _____

            E   And Isaac asked, _____

            E¹   And Abraham said, _____

         D¹   So they went *together*

      C¹   When they came to the place

           Abraham built _____

           AND laid the *wood*

           AND bound _____ and laid him on the altar

           AND reached out his _____

           AND took the _____

   B¹   The _____ spoke

A¹   Abraham _____

Based on the literary structure, what is the primary message the author wants to convey? (Hint: In a chiasm, where does the author want to draw the reader's attention?)

What comes to your mind when you think of a lamb? How would you describe the animal in terms of its appearance and temperament?

What kind of animal did Abraham see and sacrifice, according to Genesis 22:13? Contrast your image of this animal with that of a lamb.

The word ram in Hebrew is *ayil*. In addition to meaning "ram" (a mature male sheep), the word also means chief or ruler, whereas the word translated "lamb" (*seh*) simply means a young sheep or goat, either male or female.

How is Isaac's behavior presented in the text? Does it reflect characteristics more typical of a submissive lamb or of a powerful ram?

God could just as easily have provided a small lamb. Why do you suppose a ram was given instead? What might the author be trying to convey here?

Test of Faith

Reread Genesis 22:9–10.

List each step Abraham took in this passage.

Who directed Abraham's actions?

Who took charge of Isaac's role in the events?

Approximately how old is Abraham at this time?

70 to 80 years old   80 to 90 years old   90 to 100 years old   over 100 years old

Whether Isaac was a teenager or in his twenties or thirties, if he had wanted to resist Abraham, he would have had no trouble either outrunning or overpowering his elderly father; yet, he did neither.

Why do you suppose Isaac did not resist or try to run away?

Up to this point, Scripture has given us no indication that God directly communicated with Isaac. If Abraham had not been driven by complete obedience to God's will, he could never have gotten this far; and if Isaac had not acted equally in faith by submitting himself to his father's will, the entire event could never have transpired.[15] This is important because we must remember that it is Abraham's faith being tested, not Isaac's.

Read Hebrews 11:17–20.

For what is Abraham's faith commended?

What did Abraham believe God could do?

For what is Isaac's faith commended?

Scripture offers no commendation of Isaac's faith for his role in Genesis 22. Do you think this is significant? Why or why not?

List as many reasons as you can think of to explain why God may have wanted to test Abraham.

God is omniscient. He knew Abraham's heart and He certainly knew how this would all end. "The sacrifice was already accomplished in his heart, and he had fully satisfied the requirements of God."[16] God did not need, nor does He ever desire, a child sacrifice (Lev. 20:2–5; Jer. 32:35), but rather He provided an opportunity for Abraham to become fully persuaded of his own devotion to, and faith in, God. God's purpose in testing His people is never to discourage or punish them, but rather to purify and strengthen their faith.

> God's purpose in testing His people is never to discourage or punish them, but rather to purify and strengthen their faith.

Surrendering to God's Plan

PAUSE TO PONDER

Think of an occasion when you experienced a time
of testing; then answer the questions that follow. ⏀∬∽

In what ways can you relate to Abraham?

How can times of testing serve to strengthen your faith?

How might others be encouraged when they
see your unwavering faith during a time of testing?

Reread Genesis 22:11–13. In the margin, list everything Abraham does as
recorded in Genesis 22:13.

In Genesis 22:12, the Angel of the Lord once again described Isaac as "your
only son." God not only appreciated the deep love Abraham had for his son, but
He also fully understood the enormity of the sacrifice Abraham was willing to
make. Abraham's dreams had already suffered when he learned Ishmael was not
the child promised by God. If that were not painful enough, Abraham then had
to surrender his dreams for Ishmael altogether when God sent him away. Now
it appears as though God is threatening the very dream God Himself planted in
Abraham's heart: that he would become the father of a multitude of nations and
that through Isaac all the nations of the earth would be blessed. Yet we know from
Genesis 15 that Abraham "believed God" would fulfill His promises (Gen. 15:6).

Try to imagine for a moment that you are Abraham. What impact might these
events have had on his relationship with God?

Abraham believed God could raise Isaac from the dead (Heb. 11:19), but
instead, God provided a substitute. What does God's solution reveal about
His character?

Glance back at Genesis 22:8. How might the fulfillment of Abraham's own words
have served to build his faith?

Abraham did not place his hope in his own obedience, his future, his children, or his goodness, but in God and His power to raise the dead. In effect, Abraham's faith rested squarely on one thing: resurrection!

Meditate on the previous statement for a few minutes, and then share your thoughts in the margin.

Listed in the table are some things that people place their trust in (either partially or fully) to provide them with a right standing before God. Place an X next to each one that you are trusting in currently or have trusted in the past.

Abraham's faith rested squarely on one thing: resurrection!

	Previously trusted in	Currently trusting in
My obedience		
My goodness		
My children (godly parenting)		
My ministry		
Jesus		
Other: _____		
Other: _____		

Did you learn anything new about yourself? Explain.

Steps of Faith

Fill in each sentence using one of the following key words. Note: Each word is used only once.

     sacrifice   trust   build   test

Abraham struggled with the thought of letting Ishmael go free, thereby providing God an opportunity to _____ Abraham's faith.

Abraham chose to surrender Ishmael into God's care, placing his complete _____ in God.

Approximately ten to twenty years later . . .

God told Abraham to offer his son Isaac as a burnt offering, thereby putting Abraham's faith to the _____.

Abraham demonstrated his unwavering faith in God by being prepared to
_____ his son Isaac.

What observations or conclusions can you make based on these statements? ⟶

Did you notice the progression? God is loving and kind: He does not expect us to surrender to Him before we have learned to trust Him. God is also patient. He knows our fears and weaknesses: He does not put our faith to the test before it has had time to grow.

....Your Turn..

At the end of yesterday's lesson, we pondered the fact that we will encounter many mountains throughout our lives as God seeks to develop and strengthen our faith.

Yesterday, you were asked to describe the mountain you are facing right now. Thinking about your current situation, check the statement below that best reflects where you are on your mountain right now.

_____ Called to sacrifice what I hold dear

_____ In a time of testing

_____ Learning to trust God

_____ Building a foundation of faith

Take a few moments and give God praise for where you are right now. Ask Him for the courage to embrace all that He has in store for you on this journey. In the margin, write a prayer in response to what He reveals to you.

DAY FOUR
Encountering God on the Mountain

Let's begin with a quick review. In Genesis 16:13, Hagar ran away into the wilderness where she experienced a miraculous encounter with the Angel of the Lord, whom she named *El Roi*.

Write the meaning of *El Roi*.

In Genesis 16:14, we read that a well was later built there called Beer-lahai-roi, which means "The Well of the Living One Who Sees Me." The next time in Scripture we read of a location being memorialized for the miraculous intervention of God is in Genesis 22.

Reread Genesis 22:8. What does Abraham assure Isaac that God will do?

According to Genesis 22:14, what did the place come to be known as?

Let's find out if there is more going on here than meets the eye.

God Is the Same Yesterday, Today, and Tomorrow

The phrase in Genesis 16:13, "You are a God of Seeing" (also translated "You are a God Who Sees Me"), is actually made up of two Hebrew words. The first word is pronounced *el* (a shortened form of *elohim*, meaning God), and the second word is taken from the Hebrew root verb ראה (pronounced *roi*), meaning "to see". In Genesis 22:14, the Hebrew text for the phrase translated "will provide" is יְרְאֶה־ (*yireh*).

Let's look a bit closer at these two Hebrew words in the table to see what we can discover.

In the first column, trace the verb "to see" in Hebrew.

In the second column, trace the phrase "will provide" in Hebrew.

Take a few moments to compare the two Hebrew texts you have written; then, in the third column, write the Hebrew characters they have in common.

Trace the word "to see" in Hebrew:	Trace the phrase "will provide" in Hebrew:	Write the Hebrew lettering that is common in both:
ראה	יְרְאֶה־	

What conclusions can you draw based on what you observed in the tracing exercise?

The root word used in the Hebrew phrase "will provide" is ראה. It is the exact same root word used in Genesis 16:13—"roi," meaning "to see." Therefore, the literal translation of the phrase "God will provide" in Genesis 22:8 is "God will see," and in Genesis 22:14, it is "the Lord will see."

Meditate a few moments on the connection between Genesis 16 and Genesis 22. Are you encouraged? Inspired? Intrigued? Share your thoughts.

Although "will provide" is a perfectly sound and commonly accepted translation of the original text—God "saw" the need and "provided" a solution—I love the fact that Hagar's encounter in her hour of desperation with "The God Who Sees Me" is unmistakably connected by the author to the same God Abraham describes as the One who "will see" to a solution regarding the fate of his beloved son.

The Blessing of God

For the following exercise, if possible, look up the passages using the ESV translation or another version that adheres to a more literal translation (such as NASB, NKJV, or KJV). Reread the blessing God spoke over Abraham in Genesis 22:16-18. Look carefully at how the text is arranged and note anything interesting you discover.

Next, fill in the blank spaces below as they relate to the overall structure of Genesis 22:16-18. By now, you should be familiar with chiastic structure. Remember: Parallel lines may represent similar words, phrases, or concepts. I filled in the first one to get you started.

A   Abraham *obeyed* the Lord
    B   Abraham is _____ by the Lord
        C   Abraham's _____ will multiply (as the stars and sand)
            D   _____
        C¹   Through Abraham's _____ all the nations (of the earth)
    B¹   All nations will be _____
A¹   Abraham _____ the Lord

What is the key thought in this passage? Write it out in your own words.

🌿 If all the nations on earth will be blessed through Abraham and his seed, who or what might the enemies be in Genesis 22:17? List as many possibilities as you can think of.

Read 1 Peter 5:8. Who is our enemy (or adversary), according to this verse?

Read Ephesians 6:12 in the margin. Rewrite the meaning of the passage using your own words.

How can this truth encourage you when you face trials in your own life?

"For we do not wrestle against flesh and blood, but against the rulers, against the authorities, against the cosmic powers over this present darkness, against the spiritual forces of evil in the heavenly places."

—Ephesians 6:12

SUPPLEMENTAL READING

THE FAITHFULNESS OF GOD

For the past month and a half, I have struggled to write this week's lesson. Over the last few weeks, I shared with my friends my mounting frustration, feeling as if I had "hit a wall." I had no idea how true those words were about to become.

I left town to spend a few days alone with God at a friend's lovely vacation home in California's Sierra Nevada Mountains. I hoped to get caught up on my writing, but I knew I needed to be mindful that God might have other plans . . . and He did. God decided He wanted to spend our time tearing down a very old wall in my heart. To be honest, I had not realized it had become a wall. It happened quite long ago, and by this time, my emotions had grown numb.

Early the first morning, I decided to take a walk down by the lake. It was late February and the patches of snow glistened in the morning sunlight. The warmth of the sun on my face felt wonderful against the crisp mountain air. Strolling along the edge of the clear, still water, I talked silently with God about the memory He wanted me to face. I was eighteen years old at the time and was dating a man nearly ten years my senior. He was an alcoholic. One night in a fit of rage, he came after me, pinned me down, and began strangling me. Though I never knew what caused it, I will never forget the look of hatred in his eyes. Frantically, I clawed at his face. Only when I started to black out did he finally let go. I do not remember what else happened that night, but I never told anyone. Looking back, I suppose I was just too ashamed: How could I have made such a poor choice?

Walking a little further, I listened to the icy leaves crunching beneath my shoes. I paused to gaze out over the water. "Do you believe I was there that night?" God asked. His question took me by surprise. I was not a Christian at the time, so I had never thought about it before. Knowing God is everywhere at all times, I prayed silently, "Yes, God, I believe You were there." But as I rounded the far edge of the lake, I confessed to God that I still felt nothing. Then God asked me, "Why did he let go?" I paused to ponder the question, suddenly aware of a chorus of frogs croaking in the underbrush. For years, I believed he had stopped in fear of being arrested. I slowly resumed my walk and silently responded to God's question. "He let go because he got scared." Then God asked, "Who do you think scared him?" I stopped dead in my tracks. Stunned, I whispered into the still air, "It was You? It was You who saved me?" He did not need to answer; I already knew.

One night thirty years ago, the enemy of my soul used a tormented man to try to destroy me. I was just one breath away from spending all of eternity without ever knowing the love of God. And though I had not cried out a prayer or called on His name, God knew . . . and God saw . . . and God intervened. Such incredible love! Long before I ever knew Him, God protected me from entering eternity without Him. He had been there all along . . . Behind the Seen.

The Hand of God

Throughout this study, you have journeyed through some past hurts in your own life. Perhaps there is a time for which you still struggle to see how God was working Behind the Seen. All of us will face times when we want to cry out, "God, do you see me?" He is omnipresent; there is no time or place where He does not exist. And He loves you. Ask Him, and He will show you how He intervened.

The following list gives the page numbers for questions from previous weeks where you had an opportunity to invite God to help you see how He intervened in some difficult trials. Take some time right now to reexamine any questions you previously left incomplete. Prayerfully ask God to reveal how He intervened, and then fill in any questions you left blank (pages 30, 45, 62, 93, and 151).

Maybe God is bringing up a different trial you have not addressed previously. If God is revealing something new to you, ask Him to help you complete the following sentence.

When I was _____ [approximate age(s)], I felt _____
[describe how you felt, such as angry, confused, afraid or anxious, rejected,
etc.] when _____ [describe the situation].
But God _____
[describe how God revealed Himself, or protected or comforted you, or used the
events for good].

Take a few moments right now to write a prayer of thanksgiving in the margin
for the ways God has been working in your life Behind the Seen.

··Your Turn ·······································

At the end of yesterday's lesson, you marked where you are on your mountain
with God. Place an X once again that best represents where you are right now.

_____ Called to sacrifice what I hold dear

_____ In a time of testing

_____ Learning to trust God

_____ Building a foundation of faith

Is there anything keeping you from going "higher" with God? Perhaps an old
wound, unforgiveness, or fear?

What practical steps can you take to move forward in your journey with God?

　　Do you need to arrange for an extended time alone with Him?

　　Do you need to forgive someone who has hurt you?

Ask God to reveal to you what you need to do next, and then commit this to Him
in prayer. Write your prayer below.

DAY FIVE
Offering Your Dream on the Mountain

I confess: there are times when I struggle with envy, which is really just another form of idolatry. Perhaps not so coincidentally, these struggles often coincide with seasons of self-doubt. I remember once being envious of a particular Christian teacher. It was confusing for me because this person was also someone I greatly admired. On top of that, I feared people would make comparisons. What if I did not measure up?

One day as I confessed my struggles to God, He asked me this question: "Child, who put my servant on stage?" My gaze fell to the floor as I humbly answered, "You did, Lord." It was a sober reminder. As God's servants, we all belong to Him. Isaiah 64:8 teaches us that God is the One who molds us for His purposes however He sees fit. While I have grown in this area since then, I have by no means arrived. To fight this temptation, whenever I sense a hint of envy or jealousy for someone, I confess my struggle to God and then pray for the person, asking God to bless his or her ministry.

PAUSE TO PONDER

> Describe a time you envied someone—perhaps it was his or her position, possessions, or even purpose.
>
> How did you move past your struggle?
>
> If you are struggling right now, list one or two things you can do to combat envy.

Standing in the Shadows

As a slave, Hagar had spent the better part of her life living in Sarah's shadow. Whereas Sarah was known as the wife of Abraham (the future leader of God's covenant nation), Hagar was not even spoken of by name. As soon as Hagar realized she was pregnant, her true feelings reared their ugly head. "And when she saw that she had conceived, she looked with contempt on her mistress" (Gen. 16:4). We can only surmise that Hagar assumed, or at least hoped, that an elevated social status was soon to follow. Sadly, when we live our lives in someone else's shadow, it is difficult to see clearly.

"The privilege and pain of a calling come packaged together, but the calling is always a sign of God's favor." —Chris Tiegreen, from *Dancing in the Desert Devotional Bible*[17]

"O LORD, you are our Father; we are the clay, and you are our potter; we are all the work of your hand."

—Isaiah 64:8

Based on all you have learned so far, which one of the following statements is true about Hagar throughout the time she lived in Abraham's household?

She was Abraham's wife

She was the mother of the Promised Child of God

She was Sarah's slave

PAUSE TO PONDER

In what ways can envy keep us from seeing clearly?

Stepping Into the Light

Reread Genesis 17:20. List everything God promised.

Hagar's greatest aspiration was infinitely inferior to God's plan. Where Hagar may have sought "second place" in Abraham's household, God was preparing for her a place of her own: to become the mother of a mighty nation. Only after Hagar reached the end of her rope and laid down her dreams did God reveal His dream for her. "Up! Lift up the boy, and hold him fast with your hand, for I will make him into a great nation" (Gen. 21:18).

Rather than living in the shadow of Sarah, God calls Hagar to embrace a future He custom-designed just for her. A future of freedom, the beginning of her own history and heritage, and most important of all: to partner with God in His plan. God never sets us free to be left to ourselves. We are set free for one purpose: to be wholly devoted to God. And just as He did with Hagar, God may ask us to surrender our dreams—anything that threatens to distract or derail us from God's path and purpose. The reason? Because He wants us to experience something far better: to know the Living God, to love Him, and to partner with Him to accomplish His work in the world. He does not need us, of course; rather, He chooses to invite us into a holy calling.

> God never sets us free to be left to ourselves. We are set free for one purpose: to be wholly devoted to God.

The Bigger Picture

Let's step back once again in order to take a look at the bigger picture. Please reread Genesis 22:1-2 and Genesis 22:11-13; then answer the questions that follow. (Note: Some paraphrase versions of the Bible may be inadequate for the purposes of this exercise).

Who is speaking to Abraham in Genesis 22:1-2? (Be specific.) What does he tell Abraham?

Who is speaking to Abraham in Genesis 22:11-13? (Be specific.) What does he tell Abraham?

> Record anything that strikes you as interesting or unusual.

Interesting fact: The personal name for God was considered so holy that it should never be spoken out loud. It is represented by the four Hebrew consonants YHWH, which most Bibles render as LORD. YHWH is linked to the Hebrew verb *hayah*, meaning "to be," as found in Exodus 3:14, when God tells Moses, "I AM WHO I AM."

Did you notice how the author identifies the One speaking with Abraham differently in each interaction? If the author made it a point to distinguish them, it is worth our while to try to discover why. The interaction in Genesis 22:1–8 is between Abraham and God, identified in Hebrew as *Elohim*. Elohim is the more general name for God, and it first appears in Genesis 1.

Read Genesis 1:1, 3, and 26-27. (Once again: Certain paraphrase versions of the Bible may be inadequate for the purposes of this exercise.) What did God (Elohim) do? Be specific.

In contrast, Abraham's interaction with God beginning in Genesis 22:11 and throughout the rest of the chapter is with "the angel of the LORD" (or "the messenger of YHWH" in Hebrew). YHWH is the personal name of God. This name appears first in Genesis 2.

Read Genesis 2:7. What did YHWH do? Be specific.

God is both powerful and tender, infinite and intimate. God (Elohim), who spoke the world and mankind into existence (Gen. 1:27), is the same God (YHWH) who personally breathed the breath of life into Adam (Gen. 2:7). The same God

(Elohim) who spoke a command over Abraham to sacrifice his beloved son (Gen 22:2) is the same God (YHWH) who personally interceded to spare his son's life (Gen. 22:11–12).

But it gets even better!

> Compare who is speaking to Hagar in Genesis 16:7-10 with who speaks to her in Genesis 21:15-20. How does God meet Hagar's needs in each scenario?

How beautiful that the same God (Elohim) who opened Hagar's eyes and commanded her to stand up and embrace her God-given call, "Up! Lift up the boy, and hold him fast with your hand" (Gen. 21:18), is the same God (YHWH) who personally pursued her fearful, fleeing soul into the desert and comforted her with His promises (Gen. 16:7, 10).

Our View of God

> Take a few moments to ponder God in your mind. How do you envision Him? Where would you place a mark on the line below? God seems:

fearsome and distant _____ safe and intimate

> Think back on a time when life seemed to be going well. Where on the line would you have placed a mark? God seemed:

fearsome and distant _____ safe and intimate

> Thinking again about your past, when life seemed difficult or painful, where might you have placed a mark on the same line? God seemed:

fearsome and distant _____ safe and intimate

> At times when you are angry, bitter, or frustrated, where might you place a mark on the same line? God seems:

fearsome and distant _____ safe and intimate

> Lastly, when you know there is sin in your life, where might you place a mark on the same line? God seems:

fearsome and distant _____ safe and intimate

"What comes into our minds when we think about God is the most important thing about us."

—A. W. Tozer[18]

Did you learn anything new about yourself or your view of God? Explain.

PAUSE TO PONDER

What are some dangers of viewing
God as being at one extreme or the other?

God is infinite. He is as infinitely close and intimate as He is powerful and to be feared.[19] As we embrace the opportunities God provides throughout our lives to grow in our knowledge of and relationship with Him, our view of God will slowly become more balanced. However, when we find ourselves perceiving God as being at one extreme or the other, we will inevitably develop an inaccurate view not only of God, but of others and ourselves as well.

When your view of God leans too far one way or the other, what are some things you can do to bring your view of God further into balance?

Shining Light into the Darkness

Let's see how this all fits into Hagar's story. She certainly has gone through a lot, but if we focus only on the pain in her story, we will miss the greater picture. On the next few pages, we are going to retrace Hagar's struggles. For each trial she endured, we have an opportunity to step back and marvel at the blessing God orchestrated in her life.

In the table, fill in the blanks using the words provided at the top of each column.

	Trials	Blessings
	rejected separated mistreated used cast out	encounters covenant included partner hear
Genesis 12; 16:1	Hagar becomes Sarah's slave and is _____ from her people, false gods, and homeland.	BUT GOD places Hagar in a community where she would _____ of the One True God.

Day Five / Week Five

Genesis 16:2–16	Soon after Abraham and Sarah _____ Hagar to conceive a child, Hagar is _____ by Sarah.	BUT GOD pursues Hagar into the desert, where she _____ God and gives Him the name *El Roi*, the "God Who Sees Me."
Genesis 17	God reveals that Abraham and Sarah will soon have a son. Hagar's son Ishmael must therefore be _____ as the "promise child" of God.	BUT GOD safeguards Hagar and her son by ensuring that Ishmael is _____ in God's _____.
Genesis 21	Hagar and Ishmael are _____ alone into the desert, with scarcely enough provisions to last a few days.	BUT GOD saves them and invites Hagar to _____ with Him in raising up her son into a mighty nation.

Using the information you gathered in the previous table, complete the following timeline

For each period representing Hagar's approximate age, briefly describe the trial Hagar faced in the space underneath; then write the corresponding blessing in the space above each age.

I filled in the first one to get you started. Note: Age ranges are a rough estimate of what Hagar's approximate age may have been at the time of the events.

Blessings

Heard about the true God			
13 years old (Gen. 12; 16:1)	23 years old (Gen. 16:2–16)	36 years old (Gen. 17)	40 years old (Gen. 21)
Separated from homeland			

Trials

Looking at Hagar's life on the timeline, what conclusions can you draw?

At first, Hagar's story seems to leave us wanting more. I do not know about you, but I want to know how it all ends. But the reality is that nothing is missing. Hagar's story paints a beautiful picture of God's tireless pursuit to capture the heart of one wounded soul.

In what ways might Hagar's past have served to prepare her for her future?

Sometimes God leads us down a hard road not in order to make us stronger, but to bring us into a deeper and more intimate dependence on Him because it is only in Him where we find true strength. For Hagar, it is at the end of a hard road in the middle of a barren desert—the place where God dwells—that she is transformed. Remember, it was God who decided it was time to let Hagar go free (Gen. 21:12–13); however, God did not merely free Hagar *from* something. More importantly, He set her free *for* something.

"The result is that Hagar becomes the first person . . . to undergo transformation in the wilderness leading to the founding of a wilderness nation, while Moses is the second." —Thomas Dozeman[20]

For all of her pain and heartache, surrendered hopes and broken dreams, Hagar could never have imagined she would hold such a privileged place in God's plan. It would be wrong to assume that no one believed a runaway slave could ever amount to anything. God believed in her . . . and at the end of the day, that's all that mattered.

Your Turn

Ponder the mountain you are facing right now.

How might it be preparing you for God's service?

What if God's plan for your life involves a difficult test of faith, or what if it requires you to surrender a dream? Will you trust Him anyway? Will you still embrace it? Write a prayer in response to what God reveals to you.

> God does not merely free us *from* something, but more importantly, He sets us free *for* something.

> "What no eye has seen, nor ear heard, nor the heart of man imagined, what God has prepared for those who love him."
> —1 Corinthians 2:9

Lesson Summary

What Scripture, statement, or thought was most significant to you this week? Write it in the margin, and then reword it into a prayer of response to God.

There is a worship song that beautifully captures the heart of this week's lesson. It is called "In His Time" by Maranatha Singers. Perhaps you will enjoy it as well.

Notes

[1] Christopher S. Webb, "Foreword," in *A Year with God: Living Out the Spiritual Disciplines*, eds. Richard J. Foster and Julia L. Roller (New York: HarperCollins, 2009), vii.

[2] See Genesis 16:13. There are many people in Scripture who describe God or are told His name, but Hagar is the only person whom Scripture records as giving God a name.

[3] J. K. Garrett, "Moriah," in *The Lexham Bible Dictionary*, eds. J. D. Barry et al. (Bellingham, WA: Lexham Press, 2015), Logos edition.

[4] J. Strong, *New Strong's Guide to Bible Words* (Nashville: Thomas Nelson, 1997), Logos edition.

[5] J. Cornwall and S. Smith, *The Exhaustive Dictionary of Bible Names* (Alachua, FL: Bridge-Logos, 1998), 178.

[6] J. D. Currid, *A Study Commentary on Genesis*, vol. 1, *Genesis 1:1–25:18* (Darlington, England: Evangelical Press, 2003), 389.

[7] Sandra Scham, "High Place: Symbolism and Monumentality on Mount Moriah, Jerusalem," *Antiquity* 78, no. 301 (2004): 654–55.

[8] In addition to the three occurrences in Genesis 22 and the three Scriptures listed in the previous question, the other references include Judges 11:30–34 and Proverbs 4:3.

[9] J. D. Barry et al., Genesis 22:2, *Faithlife Study Bible* (Bellingham, WA: Logos Bible Software, 2012).

[10] "Idolatry," in *Nelson's New Illustrated Bible Dictionary*, ed. R. F. Youngblood (Nashville: Thomas Nelson, 1995).

[11] "Idolatry," in *Baker Encyclopedia of the Bible* , ed. W. A. Elwell (Grand Rapids, MI: Baker Book House, 1988), vol. 1, 1014.

[12] The original Hebrew text does not include the actual word "and"; rather, it includes a specific Hebrew prefix, which serves as a conjunction with the meaning of "and" or "and the."

[13] Oswald Chambers, *My Utmost for His Highest* (Grand Rapids, MI: Discovery House Publishers, 2014), January 8 entry.

[14] In addition to a sequence of words, concepts, or events, authors may also create a chiastic using a series of grammatical constructions.

[15] R. Jamieson, A. R. Fausset, and D. Brown, *Commentary Critical and Explanatory on the Whole Bible*, vol. 1 (Oak Harbor, WA: Logos Research Systems, 1997), 28–29.

[16] C. F. Keil and F. Delitzsch, *Commentary on the Old Testament*, vol. 1 (Peabody, MA: Hendrickson Publishers, 1996), 160.

[17] Chris Tiegreen, *Dancing in the Desert Devotional Bible: NLT* (Carol Stream, IL: Tyndale House Publishers, 2015), 1031.

[18] A. W. Tozer, *The Knowledge of the Holy* (New York: HarperOne, 1961), 1.

[19] "To be feared" in this context does not pertain to fear of punishment but rather relates to God as mighty, holy, and due all glory and reverence.

[20] Thomas B. Dozeman, "The Wilderness and Salvation History in the Hagar Story," *Journal of Biblical Literature* 117, no. 1 (1998): 33.

WITNESSING GOD'S PASSION

FOR THE PAST SEVERAL WEEKS, WE HAVE TRAVELED WITH Hagar along many desert roads. Then last week, we caught a glimpse of the bigger picture unfolding Behind the Seen. But in order to see the beauty of how it all ties together, we must first retrace the footprints engraved on the darkest road of all: Calvary. Whether you are well-versed in this extraordinary story or it is entirely new, if we hurry past it, we will miss the whole point of Hagar's story because all of Scripture points to Jesus.

DAY ONE
Accepting Your God-Given Assignments

Throughout our lives, each of us will face various difficulties, trials, and temptations, but there is one mountain none of us can conquer: sin.

The Problem of Sin

God loves us and desires to be in relationship with us, but He is holy and we are not. Our sin stands between us. In this regard, all of us are on equal footing. Like Isaac, we all have a death sentence on our head; like Abraham, each of us carries a burden too heavy to bear.

And just like Hagar and Ishmael in the midst of despair, our hearts cry out, *God, do you see me?* What was true for them is true for us: without God, we are helpless, hopeless, and wandering aimlessly in a barren desert while our enemy "prowls around like a roaring lion, seeking someone to devour" (1 Pet. 5:8). Then we read Genesis 22, a foreshadowing of God's plan for our deliverance, and His solution looks nothing like anything we could have imagined.

PAUSE TO PONDER

Reflect on the end of yesterday's
lesson and then complete the sentence below.

God did not merely free Hagar _____ something,

but more importantly, He set her free _____ something.

What did God free Hagar from? List
all the ways Hagar had been in slavery.

God never sets us free to be left to ourselves. We are set free for one purpose: to be wholly devoted to God.

Long before God invited Hagar to partner with Him to raise up her son into a great nation, He stretched out His hand and plucked her from a land of idolatry. Long before God fulfilled His promise to give Abraham and Sarah a son, God called Abraham away from his father's house and homeland. However, there is one promise without which none of these events would be possible. From before the world began, God bound Himself to this astonishing pledge: to come to earth on a rescue mission. All of Scripture, from Genesis to Revelation, points to this hope.

Read Matthew 20:28. What was Jesus's mission?

What comes to mind when you hear the word *ransom*? How would you describe it?

Commentator Leon Morris writes, "The word *ransom* took its origin from the practices of warfare, where it was the price paid to bring a prisoner of war out of his captivity."[1]

Reflect on this illustration. How does the idea of God paying a ransom price to free you from captivity speak to you personally?

✎ Read 1 John 2:2 and 1 Timothy 2:1-6. What do these verses reveal about God's heart?

The Problem of Religion

Roughly two thousand years have passed since Hagar and Ishmael settled in the wilderness of Paran. The scene is ancient Israel. The news of a man named Jesus is spreading, along with rumors that he may be the promised Messiah.

Imagine that you have been raised in Judaism. Year after year, you have witnessed priests offer gruesome animal sacrifices to atone for (or "cover") your sins. Then one day you are walking along the shore of the Jordan River and stop to listen to a ragged preacher named John.

Read John 1:29. How does John the Baptist describe Jesus when he sees Him approaching?

Read Exodus 12:5-7 and 12:12-13.

What kind of animal did God require to be sacrificed? Be specific.

What purpose did the sacrifice serve?

The description of the lamb being "without blemish" (or "without defect") in Exodus 12:5 is actually one word and is the same Hebrew word we studied in Genesis 17:1, where God commanded Abraham to be "blameless" (*tamin*). However, there is a problem.

Read Hebrews 10:1-4. List all of the limitations inherent in the law's sacrificial system, according to these verses.

Scripture teaches that the blood of animals is powerless to take away sins. The sacrifices simply served as a foreshadowing of what would come later. In effect, those who trusted in God's promises of forgiveness of their sins received those promises "on credit" until the true payment would be made.

God Offers a Solution

Read Matthew 3:1-6. What was John's message and what did the people do as they were being baptized?

How do the people's actions expose the limitations of the sacrificial system? (Hint: Read 1 Peter 3:21.)

Read Luke 2:52 and Matthew 3:13-17. What was spoken from heaven according to Matthew 3:17?

The Greek word commonly translated "well pleased" (*eudokesa*) in Matthew 3:17 has the idea of taking pleasure in, thinking well of, or being satisfied with. Except for the events surrounding Jesus's miraculous birth and the brief mention of the boy Jesus in the temple in Luke's Gospel (Luke 2:41–52), Scripture offers no information about Jesus's earthly life prior to His baptism. Further, His mission, as we read in Matthew 20:28, would not be accomplished for several more years.

In what way, then, might Jesus have been "pleasing" to His Father?

Where would you place an X on the line below concerning the basis of the Father's holy pleasure in Jesus?

the Father's love (for His Son) _____ what Jesus does (for His Father)

PAUSE TO PONDER

As a child of God, on what basis do you tend to
evaluate whether your heavenly Father takes
holy pleasure in you? Place an X on the line below.

my Father's love (for me) _____ what I do (for Him)

Compare your answers to the previous two questions. If they are different, why do you think that is? ❦

Read Ephesians 1:3-7.

List all of the spiritual blessings that are yours as a believer in Christ.

Which statement is true?

God chose me   I chose God

What did this choice cost, according to verse 7?

What part did you play in attracting your heavenly Father's affection?

Is there anything you are trying to do now to earn His affection? If so, how might this grieve the heart of God? ❦

Satan Offers a Shortcut

Read Matthew 4:1-7.

What comes to mind when you think of the word *temptation*? How would you describe it?

Glance back at Genesis 21:12-16. Compare and contrast this passage with Matthew 4:1-4. List any similarities you discover.

Glance back at Genesis 22:1-2. Compare and contrast this passage with Matthew 4:5-7. List any similarities you discover.

Listed in the table are various details included in all three accounts. I completed the first column for you. In the second and third columns, place an X underneath each column if the detail is also represented in that story.

Detail	Hagar & Ishmael (Genesis 21:12-16)	Abraham & Isaac (Genesis 22:1-2)	Jesus (Matthew 4:1-7)
Sent by the will of God (or Spirit of God)	X		
Went alone (or together, but alone)	X		
Wilderness (or desert)	X		
Bread	X		
Testing / temptation			
Moriah / site of the holy city			

 What conclusions can you draw from this table?

SUPPLEMENTAL READING

"DON'T GIVE THE DEVIL SO MUCH CREDIT"

"Don't give the devil so much credit."

I do not remember the exact details that prompted my friend to say such a thing, but I do recall being a young believer at the time. I was struggling with something that was not going my way. Ever been there? I carelessly blamed my difficulty on the schemes of the devil, which prompted my friend's gentle correction: "Don't give the devil so much credit."

It is so easy—even tempting—to assume every trial we face is rooted in the enemy's schemes. He is delighted, of course, for this focuses our attention onto ourselves and our problems, and away from God, providing fertile ground for the enemy to plant seeds of doubt in our minds as to God's goodness, power, or love.

What if we are giving the devil too much credit? Is every struggle we encounter really from the enemy?

I wrestled with these questions, so I did some research. I discovered that in the New Testament, the Greek word translated temptation is *peirasmos*; it is the same word translated as testing. Even more curious, the word stems from the Greek word *peira*, which means "an experiment." *Isn't that comforting?* The word itself is neutral; the interpretation depends on the context. If Satan is attempting to entice a person to sin, it is translated as temptation. However, if God is orchestrating events in order to strengthen a person's faith, build his character, or serve some other godly purpose, then it is translated as testing.

"Beloved, do not be surprised at the fiery trial when it comes upon you to test you . . ." (1 Peter 4:12).

No one wants to suffer trials, but Scripture clearly teaches that there are times when God allows them for His good purposes.

"You meant evil against me, but God meant it for good" (Gen. 50:20).

While we may not understand why God does everything that He does, He has, in His grace, revealed to us who He is. He is loving, holy, patient, all-knowing, good, and so much more. These are the truths we must cling to whenever we suffer and are tempted to doubt our heavenly Father's wisdom, goodness, or love.

When we face trials, may we resolve to trust in God's revelation of Himself, and if we must suffer, to trust God will even empower us to rejoice (even "to boast")[2] in our suffering (Rom. 5:1–5).

Jesus understands our struggles. Like Hagar and Ishmael in the wilderness, Jesus suffered hunger; Jesus suffered thirst. Like Abraham and Isaac on Mount Moriah, Jesus was also put to the test. And in every scenario, it was God who led them there.

Read Hebrews 4:15 in the margin. How would you describe the notion that Jesus *"in every respect* has been tempted as we are" (emphasis mine)?

"For we do not have a high priest who is unable to sympathize with our weaknesses, but one who in every respect has been tempted as we are, yet without sin."

—Hebrews 4:15

This verse is quoted often, but it is sometimes misunderstood. Scripture teaches that Jesus is both fully man and fully God (John 1:1, 14). As God, he is holy and therefore could never be enticed to sin. But this then begs the question:

How can the author say that Jesus was "tempted" as we are "in every way"? We will explore this question tomorrow by carefully unpacking the Scripture as well as examining in greater detail the specific temptations Jesus faced. Until then, let us take a moment to review what we have learned so far and see how it applies to our own lives.

PAUSE TO PONDER

Earlier in today's lesson, we reviewed this truth:
God did not merely free Hagar from something,
but more importantly, He set her free for something.

In the margin, rewrite the above sentence;
however, in place of Hagar's name, insert your own.

What has God freed you from? Reflecting on
your life, list all of the ways you have been in slavery.

If you are a child of God, the mountain of sin that stood between you and God has been removed. You are no longer a slave to sin (Rom. 6:6) and can rest in the security of your Father's love. It is from within this relationship that God invites you to partner with Him to experience joy and fulfillment as you serve Him by serving others.

Recall from memory how Jesus described His mission by completing the following sentence: "The Son of Man came not to be _____ but to _____, and to give His life as a ransom for many." (Hint: Matthew 20:28.)

································Your Turn································

List the various people in your inner circle that God has positioned you to serve at this particular time in your life, such as your spouse, boss, coworkers, children, co-laborers in ministry, and so on.

Where do you to struggle the most to follow Jesus's example of being willing to serve rather than be served?

How has the enemy tried to entice you to claim your "rights" over serving the needs of this person?

How may God be calling you to surrender your rights in order to serve the needs of this person? What would it look like? Be specific.

List one thing you will do this week to serve this person. Write a prayer of commitment below.

DAY TWO
Standing Firm against the Enemy

Yesterday, we ended our lesson by briefly examining Hebrews 4:15. Like any passage of Scripture, context is key.

Read Hebrews 3:1. How are the recipients of the letter described? Is the author describing believers in Christ or nonbelievers?

When studying Scripture, why is it important to understand who the author is writing to?

Read Hebrews 2:1, 3:12, and 4:14. What is the author's concern, according to these verses?

The Problem of Temptation

For those of us living in the modern West, we often associate temptation with things that stem from sinful desires, such as lust, pride, greed, or envy. However, as we just examined, these kinds of temptations are not what the author of Hebrews

> "For we do not have a high priest who is unable to sympathize with our weaknesses, but one who in every respect has been tempted as we are, yet without sin."
> —Hebrews 4:15

is concerned about. Therefore, in order to better understand Hebrews 4:15, we need to take a closer look at the three temptations Jesus endured in the wilderness.

Reread Matthew 4:1–10. How does Satan describe Jesus?

Interesting Fact: Messiah and Christ both mean "anointed," which signifies kingship. Messiah is a title derived from the Hebrew *mashiach*, a verbal adjective meaning "anointed one"; the word *Christ* is the Greek equivalent.[3]

This is the first occurrence of this expression used to address Jesus in the Bible. Satan very well could have challenged Jesus's identity as the Messiah (or the Christ), but he did not. It makes me cringe to think that the first occurrence of this title, which beautifully depicts the intimacy Jesus shared with the Father,[4] was when Satan sneered, "If you are the Son of God . . ."

Recall from yesterday's lesson: What was Jesus's mission? (Hint: Reread Matthew 20:28.)

Keeping in mind the temptations of Jesus in Matthew 4, look up the following Scriptures; then fill in the sentences with a word of your choice that best completes each thought.

John 6:35   Philippians 2:8   Matthew 9:35

Jesus did not come to feed Himself, but to become _____ for others.

Jesus did not come to exalt Himself, but to _____ Himself and lay down His life for others.

Jesus did not come to crown Himself, but to bring the good news of the _____ to others.

Meditate on these statements for a few moments. Which one stands out to you the most? Why?

Satan's Challenge: God's Timing

None of the temptations Jesus endured stemmed from evil desires. After forty days, Jesus suffered hunger. To want to satisfy hunger is not sin (Matt. 6:11). He is also the Savior who came to earth to draw all people to Himself (John 12:32). To want the people He created and loved to know who He was is not sin (and a leap off the top of the temple would surely get their attention). Finally, Jesus is King of kings and Lord of lords (Dan. 7:13–14 and Rev. 19:16).[5] For Him to want to establish justice and reclaim rule over the earth, which rightfully belongs to Him, is not sin.

However, for Jesus to act on any of these truths in a manner or at a time that is not in alignment with His Father's will *would* be sin. In effect, it would have been unbelief: doubting His Father's goodness, His wisdom, or His love.

PAUSE TO PONDER

Think of a time you were tempted to pursue something good, but in the wrong time or wrong way. How is this unbelief?

Read Matthew 16:15-16, 21-23. Compare and contrast this scene with Matthew 4:10 and then answer the questions that follow.

Given Peter's desire to follow Jesus (Matt. 14:29), what may have prompted Peter to say what he said in Matthew 16:22?

According to Jesus, what was the underlying cause of Peter's error?

What effect did Peter's words have on Jesus?

What can you learn from this interaction? What principle(s) can you apply to your own life?

Satan knew that if Jesus fulfilled His mission, his own sinister reign of darkness would come to an end. It should be no surprise, then, that Satan would stop at nothing to try and derail Jesus. On the surface, it appears Satan's questions are challenging Jesus's identity, and in one sense he is, for Jesus's identity and authority are inseparable.

However, Satan knows full well who Jesus is.[6] His sneering words, *If you are the Son of God,* are an attempt to provoke Jesus. Satan *wants* Jesus to use His divine privileges. Satan knows that if Jesus were to use His supernatural power outside of His Father's will, He would forfeit His mission[7] to live and die as the Son of Man.

As Jesus wrestles under the weight of humanity's limitations, Satan strikes with venomous words that simultaneously attack Jesus and blaspheme God.

Satan's Challenge: God's Goodness

Is your Father not willing to feed you?
Will He not protect you?
Hasn't He promised that you will rule the earth?
(Ps. 2, particularly verses 7 and 8.)

These are seeds of doubt that Satan attempts to plant in Jesus's mind. Again, Satan knows the truth. He knows who God is. He even knows God's words and quotes them; however, he does so in an attempt to get Jesus to play into his hands. Jesus prevails against every temptation because He is anchored in three things.

Match each phrase below with the word that best describes it by drawing a line between each pair.

Jesus knew who He was.	Humility
Jesus knew the Word of God.	Identity
Jesus was determined to obey His Father's will.	Authority

PAUSE TO PONDER

Which area do you tend to struggle with the most?

My identity as a beloved child of God

Trusting in the authority of God's Word

Obedience or surrender to God's will

Why do you suppose this is a difficult area for you?

How might the enemy use this to
gain a foothold in your walk with God?

When the author of Hebrews writes that Jesus can sympathize with our weaknesses because "in every respect [He] has been tempted as we are," he is not suggesting that Christ endured every possible human temptation there is to experience, but rather that He experienced "in every way the full force of our temptation yet without yielding to it."[8]

As a matter of fact, for Satan to try to rouse evil desires in Jesus would be wasted effort. Jesus is the Son of God. He is holy and therefore cannot be tempted by evil (James 1:13).[9] But one thing is certain: Jesus suffered under tremendous temptation. As we learned earlier, not all temptations are rooted in desire for evil things. In fact, the underlying source of those kinds of temptations may surprise you.

> Read James 1:13-14. Who or what causes us to be tempted "by evil"? Does this surprise you? Why or why not?

The Victory over Temptation

Some may argue that Jesus, who was born without our propensity to sin, cannot sympathize with our weaknesses or be our example to follow. But this line of thinking mistakenly equates humanness with sinfulness, when in fact sin is a pollutant. In the beginning, God created mankind in His own image (Gen. 1:27). When Adam and Eve were tempted, "being tempted" in and of itself, was not sin. Rather, it was not until they chose to disobey God that sin entered humankind, passing from them to all generations (Rom. 5:12–19). Jesus, however, was conceived not by a human father, but by the Holy Spirit, and therefore did not inherit Adam's sin.

Jesus was also fully human (John 1:14, Rom. 1:3, Phil. 2:7–8, Heb. 2:14). He suffered hunger, thirst, pain—even death. He knew sorrow, anguish, and grief. He suffered tremendous temptation beyond what any human being has ever suffered since the beginning of time . . . yet never sinned.

> Read 1 Corinthians 10:13.
>
> What are the only two possible outcomes for a believer who is being tempted?

> Which of these options, if any, did Jesus experience?

> What conclusions can you draw?

When you and I are tempted, we will do one of two things: take the way of escape before it passes us by, or cave in to sin. In either case, we never endure the full measure of the temptation. Not so for Jesus. He never backed out and He never caved in. Therefore, He is the only One who ever suffered temptation to its complete end. This is why He can sympathize with our weaknesses. He fought and fought and fought and resisted the full measure of Satan's attacks—not just in the wilderness, but all the way to the Cross—even to His last breath, knowing that He could have stopped it all at any moment with just . . . one . . . word.

But He did not. He endured it all—not in His divine power—but in His humanity (that is, His flesh), and the indwelling power of the Holy Spirit. This is why He can serve as our example to follow when we are born again and likewise begin to live by the indwelling power of the Holy Spirit. Although at times we will still struggle and fail (Rom. 7:23), with the power of the Holy Spirit living within us, we can actually choose not to sin (Rom. 6:6; 1 John 3:9, Ezek. 36:27, Gal. 5:16, Phil. 2:13).

How has exploring the context of Hebrews 4:15 furthered your understanding of this verse?

Your Three Anchors

Jesus prevailed over the enemy because He had full confidence in who He was, depended on the authority of God's Word, and was fully surrendered to His Father's will. Likewise, our victory depends on being anchored in these same three things:

- Our identity—a beloved child of God
- Our authority—the Word of God
- Our humility—surrendered to the will of God

And just as Satan challenged Jesus, "If you are the Son of God . . . ," he will challenge us, "If you are a child of God. . . ." Satan knows our identity and the full weight of God's authority behind it. The question is: Do we?

.................................Your Turn ....

What one step will you take this week to further anchor these three truths in your mind and heart?

Commit your action step to God in prayer. Write your prayer in the margin.

If you are a child of God, the enemy no longer has any claim on you. He also knows that your prayers, when aligned with God's will as revealed in His Word, have authority because Jesus is our great high priest who "always lives to make intercession for [us]" (Heb. 4:14; 7:25). "Let us then with confidence draw near to the throne of grace, that we may receive mercy and find grace to help in time of need" (Heb. 4:16).

DAY THREE
Aligning Your Will to God's Plan

From the first Garden paradise of Eden, humans have struggled with trials and temptations, sin and Satan, and have been in desperate need of deliverance. Then, in another Garden in another time, just when it seemed God was about to answer—instead of deliverance, disaster struck.

Prophecy Unfolding before Their Eyes

By the time Jesus arrives on the scene, the Jews have suffered under Roman rule for close to one hundred years. Israel's succession of kings have come and gone. And while the Jewish people have been eagerly awaiting their Messiah, Jesus's arrival does not usher in the freedom in the way they had hoped.

> Read Matthew 21:1-11. List everything the prophet says about the one he sees coming, according to verse 5.[10]

After Jesus enters His beloved city Jerusalem with crowds of people dancing and singing all around Him, He heads toward the temple. Regarding this ascension, theologian R. C. Sproul writes that "ascending" was "connected to the enthronement after victory, when the spoils of battle would be brought up to God's house and captives from the battle would be led through the city. This reference to captives is not a description of Satan, but to Christ's people whom Christ defeated in the sense of destroying their sins and setting them free. He presented the train, comprising his people, to the Father."[11]

However, this freedom would come at a high price.

"And when the devil had ended every temptation, he departed from him *until an opportune time*" (Luke 4:13; emphasis mine).

Events Unfolding Behind the Seen

Read Matthew 26:1–16 at least two times all the way through (read it at least one time out loud). What parallels or contrasts can you discover?

In the table, I have listed various parallels and contrasts taken from the passage. Fill in the blanks based on what you learned in your reading. I included extra space at the end of the table for any additional parallels you discovered. I completed a few to get you started.

Jesus prophesies He will be _crucified_ on _Passover_	The chief priests and elders want to avoid _killing_ Jesus on _Passover_
House of Simon the _____	_____ of Caiaphas the _____ _____
The woman _planned_ an act of _worship_	The men _____ an act of _____ _____
Alabaster jar of very _____ perfume (worth a year's wages or 300 denarii; Mark 14:5)	They paid him _____ pieces of silver (about a month's wages, the price to compensate an owner for a slave's death; Exod. 21:32)
The woman _gave_ a gift	Judas asked, "What will you _____ _____ if I deliver him?"
The _____ were _indignant_	The chief priests and elders feared a(n) _____
Jesus describes the woman's act as _____ _____	Jesus's _____ describe the woman's act as _____

How do these contrasts contribute to your understanding or appreciation of the text?

Compare and contrast Matthew 26:24 with Matthew 26:13. How seriously does Jesus view a person's devotion or rejection of Him?

What implications does this have for our own lives? ⚜

An Extravagant Gift

The woman is Mary of Bethany, the sister of Lazarus and Martha. After breaking the wax seal of her alabaster jar and all cultural norms, Mary lovingly empties its contents, anointing Jesus's head with the fragrant oil.[12] A jar of this kind would typically contain about twelve ounces, allowing the oil to flow all the way to Jesus's feet (John 12:3).

Mary's act was far more than a kind gesture of respect and adoration. The gift was equivalent to a whole year's salary and possibly tied to her hope for marriage —her hope for a future. It was often saved for a young woman's wedding day, when she would pour it on her husband as an act of devotion (see Song of Sol. 1:12 in the margin).

Mary gave Jesus the most precious thing she owned—with no hope of any return in this life. Yet only One noticed the value of her extravagant gift: Jesus. Where the disciples saw a fool, Jesus saw a worshiper. What the disciples called a waste, Jesus received as a gift. Jesus saw Mary's heart. He saw Behind the Seen. Jesus was so taken by her selfless act that He declared her actions would be proclaimed for all eternity.

> "While the king was at his table, my perfume gave forth its fragrance"
> —Song of Solomon 1:12 NASB

PAUSE TO PONDER

Only Jesus saw the value of Mary's gift. How can this encourage you when others chastise you for your service or devotion to God? ⚜

A Greater Purpose

What specific purpose did Mary's actions serve, according to Jesus's own words in Matthew 26:12?

There is no consensus among scholars as to whether Mary understood the true purpose of her actions. Nevertheless, most contend that the Holy Spirit led her there that night.

Read the following verses: Acts 2:23; 1 Peter 1:19-20; Matthew 16:21. Who is ultimately orchestrating these events: man or God?

When you think of Jesus's walk to Calvary, do you tend to view Him as a victim or a volunteer? Explain. *Ꮨ*

When events in your own life and the world around you seem to go against all that is right and good, how can you take comfort in knowing that God is always in control? *Ꮨ*

An Exaggerated Claim

Read Matthew 26:26-46.

Only four days[13] after joyful crowds surrounded Jesus with songs and praises, Jesus stepped into the lonely Garden of Gethsemane. Within hours, He would be surrounded by a hateful mob wielding swords and clubs.

*Center your attention on Matthew 26:30-35. Consider the predictions Jesus makes with the claims Peter makes in this passage. Now read Matthew 16:21-22. What conclusions can you draw?

Jesus knows that

what we need most

is not correction, but

resurrection!

No one wants to be discovered a liar. Even more, no one wants to declare God a liar. Yet Peter does both without even realizing it—again. Even more astounding is the fact that Jesus does not engage Peter and the other disciples in an ongoing debate. Peter loved Jesus, and his intentions were sincere, yet Jesus knew what Peter and the other disciples did not understand: what they needed most was not correction, but resurrection. Jesus placed no faith in what they could do, but He had full faith in what He could do. This is why Jesus could confidently say to them, "But after I am raised up, I will go before you to Galilee."

The Divine Will

Center your attention on Matthew 26:36–46; then answer the questions that follow.

What was Jesus's first request when He prayed to His Father?

How does this compare to His second and third prayers? What changed?

Read Mark 14:36. What additional detail is included here?

Do you think this is significant? Why or why not?

Matthew 26:39 tells us that Jesus "fell on his face and prayed." Sproul writes, "In the ancient world the Jews would pray standing up and looking to heaven. Jesus on this occasion broke with that tradition; the burden of his prayer was so heavy and it bore down on him so much so that he sank to his knees to pray."[14]

Read Luke 22:44 in the margin. Is there any indication that Jesus wanted to suffer the death He was about to suffer? Explain.

> "And being in agony he prayed more earnestly; and his sweat became like great drops of blood falling down to the ground."
>
> —Luke 22:44

As blood, sweat, and tears poured forth from Jesus's body, something else penetrated the veil of darkness that night: the sweet aroma of Mary's perfume.

Jesus was not afraid of death. He said to His disciples all along that He came to earth to die.[15] He even declared that Mary's precious anointing was preparation for His burial. But the suffering leading up to death is a different story. Jesus's agony in the garden was His wrestling with His Father as to whether He could endure all that would be required of Him: physically, mentally, and most of all, spiritually. Jesus would have to bear the full weight—and punishment—for the world's sin.

As in the wilderness where after forty days without food or water Jesus was most vulnerable, here was the "opportune time" Satan had been waiting for. The enemy knew he had no power over the Son of God, *but the Son of Man*—Jesus's humanity—had not been fully tested. Satan's temptations in the wilderness may have failed, but when Jesus fell on His face with sweat and blood dripping from His skin, surely Satan slithered up beside Him, seeking any opportunity to destroy Jesus's resolve.

Yet even in the midst of intense temptation, Jesus was never tempted to disobey His Father, but rather prayed at first that His Father's will would be different.[16] Jesus never ceased for one moment being fully divine and, as Son of God, His will could never be in conflict with God the Father. Nevertheless, being also fully human, Jesus dreaded the suffering He was about to endure.

The Dire Warning

In Matthew 26:41, we read that Jesus warned His disciples.

Write Jesus's warning below.

How can we protect ourselves from temptation, according to Jesus?

> "You have taken away my companions and loved ones. Darkness is my closest friend."
>
> —Psalm 88:18 NLT

Just as Jesus battled Satan's temptations alone in the wilderness, Jesus was left alone in His agony in the garden. Although Jesus asked His friends to "stay awake" and "watch with me," they could not. Commentary author Dr. Robert Hawker writes, "Jesus himself said, that this was the hour of the enemies' triumph, and the powers of darkness; and it seems more than probable, that *Satan* had drenched those few faithful servants of the Lord ill with stupidity and heaviness to sleep on purpose, that all human comfort should be withdrawn at this awful time from Christ; and Christ left alone to combat in this unparalleled struggle!"[17]

There is one consistent plea in all three of Jesus's prayers. What was it?

.....................................Your Turn.....................................

Think of a time when you brought a difficult matter to God repeatedly through prayer (perhaps you are wrestling with God about something right now). What point on the line best represents your initial approach to prayer?

desiring God to conform ———————————————— desiring to conform
His will to mine   my will to God's

When you reached the end of your prayers, what point on the line best represents your final approach in prayer?

desiring God to conform ———————————— desiring to conform
    His will to mine   my will to God's

Did your approach change? Share your thoughts.

What can you learn from Jesus's example?

How does the fact that Jesus repeatedly went to His Father in heartrending prayer—not once, but three times—encourage you personally?

DAY FOUR
Preparing to Enter Enemy Territory

We have certainly covered a lot of material these past weeks. Take several moments right now to appreciate how hard you have worked and how far you have come. Please know I am praying for you and cheering you on as you press forward on this journey.

Before we dive into today's lesson, I have a personal story to share with you. It is not one I was eager to write, but after wrestling with God about it for some time, I knew what I had to do.

The Sting of Words

I had been with my former husband more than ten years when a recession hit in the late 1990s. After nearly a year without work, we moved across the country where the economy seemed brighter. Although we were far from New York where we both grew up, in no time at all we found new jobs, settled into an apartment, and began to make new friends. It did not take long before one of these friends invited us to church. Having no faith or church background to speak of, I never could have imagined that within just a few months, I would give my heart to Jesus. However, rather than bringing peace and healing to my marriage, my new faith wasn't able to keep our deep-seated problems from growing worse.

"The tongue . . . is a restless evil, full of deadly poison."
—James 3:8

At one point, we agreed to be counseled by a pastor and his wife. During a private session between me and the pastor's wife, I was advised to go home and do one of the hardest things I have ever been asked to do: to put the past behind me and give myself anew to my husband. I never felt more vulnerable. To be truthful, my efforts were not as much motivated by romantic love as by a sincere desire to do things God's way.[18] It took every last ounce of courage I had. That night, I turned to my husband in the quiet darkness, expecting we would begin the long process of healing. But rather than a tender kiss, a sting was my reward.

"No thanks."

The words cut deeply. The poison quickly burrowed deep into my heart: *I don't want you. I don't love you. You are not worth fighting for.*

Oftentimes, the sting of words provides fertile ground for the most poisonous lies.

PAUSE TO PONDER

Ponder the previous sentence for a few
moments. Do you agree? Why or why not?

The Kiss

So far in this study, we have examined the first occurrence of the words *love*, *only*, and *worship*. We are now going to explore another first. However, rather than setting a tone, this story sets the stage. To see how the scene plays out, we will skip back to Genesis to read a story about Abraham's son Isaac and his adult twin sons. You will not have to answer any questions for this one. Just sit back, relax, and open your Bible to the book of Genesis.

Read Genesis 25:19–34 and 27:1–27.

Abraham's son Isaac is now old and nearing his death. He is the father of Esau, his firstborn and favored son, and Jacob, Esau's twin brother, who is favored by their mother, Rebekah (Gen. 25:28). As we learned in Week Four of this study, in Old Testament times, the firstborn son often enjoyed special privileges and inheritance rights. Jacob is well aware of this when Esau forfeits his birthright in exchange for a steamy bowl of stew. Years later, Rebekah decides to cook up a plan of her own. After a brief discussion concerning whether he could pull off such a hoax, Jacob's willingness to conspire with his mother, deceive his father, and betray his brother culminates in . . . one . . . simple . . . kiss.

This is the first mention of a kiss in Scripture, but it would not be the last. How tragic that what God created to serve as a tender expression of love first appears in Scripture as a vile act of betrayal.

Beware: The "Frenemy"

Every so often a new word is added to our dictionaries, such as *frenemy*, a slang word combining "friend" with "enemy."

> What comes to mind when you hear the word frenemy? If this term is new to you, simply write your best guess of what the word might mean, given its composition.

According to dictionary.com, a frenemy is described as "a person or group that is friendly toward another because the relationship brings benefits, but harbors feelings of resentment or rivalry."

> Read Matthew 26:47-68. Center your attention on Matthew 26:47-50; then answer the questions that follow.

> What was the betrayer's relationship to Jesus and how did he act toward Jesus?

> How does Jesus address His betrayer, and what does this reveal about God's character?

Beware: Your Friends

> Center your attention on Matthew 26:51-56; then answer the questions that follow.

> Suppose the disciples had succeeded in fighting off the crowd and preventing Jesus's arrest. How might their actions have served Satan's agenda? (Hint: Glance back at Matthew 16:21-23.)

"Faithful are the wounds of a friend; profuse are the kisses of an enemy."

—Proverbs 27:6

What could Jesus have done, according to Matthew 26:53?

In the end, what did the disciples do?

Read John 16:32 in the margin. Knowing all that would soon happen, what truth does Jesus claim for Himself before the events unfold?

"Behold, the hour ... has come, when you will be scattered ... and will leave me alone. Yet I am not alone, for the Father is with me." —John 16:32

What can you learn from Jesus's example?

Beware: The Religious

Reread Matthew 26:57–68. List everything Jesus endured at the hands of "the religious."

In a typical modern-day courtroom in the Western world, when a person is placed on trial, what is the intent or aim of the proceedings?

What was the intent for bringing Jesus before the chief priests and the council, according to Matthew 26:59?

Compare your responses to the last two questions. What conclusions can you make?

Just three days after Jesus's Triumphal Entry into Jerusalem, He is betrayed by a frenemy, abused by the religious, and abandoned by His friends.

PAUSE TO PONDER

Which of the experiences of Jesus have
you suffered personally? Circle all that apply.

wounds of a "frenemy"
wounds of a friend   wounds from "the religious"

Think of a time when you or someone you loved suffered
one of these wounds. How can you take comfort in
knowing that Jesus likewise suffered in this way?

Many of us can recall being on the receiving end of wounds inflicted by another. However, if we are honest with ourselves, there are times when we also have been tempted to walk in their shoes. Perhaps befriending a coworker in order to better position ourselves at work. Or breaking a promise to a friend when they needed us. Especially as Christians, we can easily inflict injury with our careless self-righteousness. At the root of all of these temptations are the sins of pride and unbelief. Pride (an inflated or false view of self) and unbelief (a degraded or false view of God) are like two sides of the same ugly coin.

Explain or give an example of what pride and unbelief might look like in each of the following scenarios. I filled in two to get you started.

Scenario	What might pride look like? (Inflated or false view of self)	What might unbelief look like? (Degraded or false view of God)
Being a "frenemy"		
Being an unreliable friend	Breaking my promise to watch my friend's children when another friend calls offering tickets to a popular event the same night	
Being self-righteous		Thinking that God is more impressed by what I do or say than what I really think or feel

Which of the following temptations have you succumbed to personally? Circle all that apply.

being a "frenemy"   being an unreliable friend   being self-righteous

How can you guard yourself against these temptations?

Beware: The Human Heart

Compare and contrast Luke 22:31–34 with Matthew 26:69–75. What did Peter discover about himself?

> "The heart is deceitful
> above all things."
> —Jeremiah 17:9a

God knows our hearts better than we do. Peter believed the words he spoke to Jesus, but Jesus knew that apart from God's power, Peter's words were altogether empty. Jesus Himself told Peter (and reminds us as well) that "the spirit indeed is willing, but the flesh is weak" (Matt. 26:41).

At the start of this week's lesson, we began with this truth: "Without God, we are helpless, hopeless, wandering aimlessly in a barren desert all the while our enemy 'prowls around like a roaring lion, seeking someone to devour'" (1 Pet. 5:8). So how do we protect ourselves? To answer this question, we need to read this verse in its context.

Read 1 Peter 5:6–11.

List everything we are told to do, according to these verses.

How did Jesus model this for us?

As long as we live in enemy territory, we should not be surprised that the enemy will do everything he can to try to derail us through deception, temptation, condemnation, and anything else that provides him a foothold in our thoughts. Satan knows it is our thoughts that determine our actions.

Read the Scriptures listed below. What common principles can you discover?

1 Peter 1:13–16   2 Corinthians 10:4–5   Colossians 3:1–3

Read at least two of the following passages (1 Peter 5:6–11 is a review). Based on these verses, what do we risk by failing to set our minds on God's truth?

Romans 8:5–8   Romans 12:1–2   Philippians 4:4–8   1 Peter 5:6–11

Because Scripture teaches that even our own hearts betray us (Jer. 17:9a), as Christians, we must make it our habit to continually renew our minds by meditating on God's Word and yielding our lives to the leading of the Holy Spirit dwelling within us. When we do not, we risk:

- Becoming anxious (Phil. 4:6)
- Being an easy target for the enemy (1 Pet. 5:8)
- The inability to discern God's will (Rom. 12:2)
- An inability to please God (Rom. 8:8)
- Becoming conformed to the world's philosophies (Rom. 12:2)
- Our minds becoming hostile toward God (Rom. 8:7)

Which of these have you experienced personally? Circle all that apply.

Why is meditating on God's Word so important? *Off~*

"The spirit indeed is willing, but the flesh is weak."

—Matthew 26:41

......................Your Turn ....

Reread Matthew 26:41 in the margin. How are you currently experiencing this truth in your own life right now? (Keep in mind that our "flesh" also includes our thoughts and feelings.)

What would it look like for you to have victory in this area?

What one truth from God's Word will you set your mind on this week? Write it down here as well as on a note card to keep with you as a reminder.

DAY FIVE
Clinging to God in Your Darkest Hour

He was despised and rejected by men,
    a man of sorrows, and acquainted with grief;
and as one from whom men hide their faces
    he was despised, and we esteemed him not.
Surely he has borne our griefs and carried our sorrows;
    yet we esteemed him stricken, smitten by God, and afflicted.
But he was pierced for our transgressions;
    he was crushed for our iniquities;
upon him was the chastisement that brought us peace,
    and with his wounds we are healed. (Isa. 53:3–5)

Despised and Rejected by Men

Given mankind's rebellion against God since the Garden of Eden, perhaps there is no greater understatement in all of Scripture than the words, "He was despised and rejected by men."

Read Matthew 27:1-50.

List every person or group that insulted or condemned Jesus with words.

How do those who pass by challenge Jesus's identity? What do they say in Matthew 27:40?

Do those words sound familiar? Recall the first time this title is used for Jesus, and describe the scenario. (Hint: Glance back at Matthew 4:1-3.)

How else was Jesus ridiculed, according to Matthew 27:41-43?

"He was despised and rejected by men."
—Isaiah 53:3

⌇ Compare Matthew 4:6 with Matthew 27:40-43. How may the mockers' words have further contributed to Jesus's misery?

Pierced for Our Transgressions

Describe all that Jesus suffered physically as recorded in Matthew 27:26-31 and 35.

The torture of Jesus's crucifixion seems almost glossed over in Scripture. There are simply no words to describe all that Jesus endured. Artists who depict Jesus on the Cross often downplay the extent of His wounds and out of respect include a garment. The reality is that Jesus was beaten and bloodied (Matt. 27:26; Isa. 52:14), and criminals were stripped naked and then crucified.[19] Commentary author Dr. Robert Hawker draws a forceful parallel when he writes, "[Just] as Adam had made himself naked by sin, so CHRIST, in removing the curse, condescends to this shame . . . to do away [with] sin by the sacrifice of himself."[20]

What thoughts or feelings come to mind when you consider how Jesus suffered such shame on our behalf?

PAUSE TO PONDER

Read Romans 10:11. How does this truth speak to you personally? ⌇

Read Luke 23:33-34.

How did Jesus respond to the soldiers who crucified Him? Write Jesus's words in the margin.

What does Jesus's prayer reveal about God's heart?

How can Jesus's response to the soldiers encourage you when you realize you have offended or grieved God? ⌇

Man of Sorrows

Using the words provided, fill in each blank with the person or persons responsible for Jesus's suffering, according to what we read this week in Matthew 26 and 27. I have provided the Scripture references if you want to check your responses. Note: Some words may be used more than once.

Pilate   soldiers   crowd   scribes   Judas
thieves   disciples   Peter   elders

_____ betrayed Jesus for thirty pieces of silver. (Matt. 26:14–16)

The _____ abandoned Jesus in the Garden of Gethsemane. (Matt. 26:56)

At the palace of Caiaphas the high priest, the _____ and _____ abused Jesus. (Matt. 26:57, 65–68)

_____ denied Jesus three times. (Matt. 26:69–75)

The _____ rejected Jesus in place of a murderer. (Matt. 27:15, 20–23)

_____ had Jesus scourged (flogged/whipped). (Matt. 27:24–26)

Then, _____ condemned Jesus to death (by handing Him over to be crucified). (Matt. 27:24–26)

Using a crown of thorns, the _____ mocked Jesus. (Matt. 27:27–31)

The _____ crucified Jesus at a place called Golgotha. (Matt. 27:31–36)

Two _____, one on His right and the other on His left, reviled Jesus. (Matt. 27:38, 44)

For each fill-in sentence, circle the action verb.

Next, using the action verbs you just circled, plot Jesus's suffering on the following timeline. I completed two to get you started.

		abused		scourged					
Matt. 26:14–16	Matt. 26:56	Matt. 26:57, 65–68	Matt. 26:69–75	Matt. 27:15, 20–23	Matt. 27:24–26	Matt. 27:24–26	Matt. 27:27–31 †	Matt. 2:31–36	Matt. 27:38, 44

PAUSE TO PONDER

> How can reflecting on Jesus's walk to Calvary comfort you in times when you feel that no one understands your sorrow or suffering?

"My God, my God, why have you forsaken me?"

—Psalm 22:1

Forsaken by God

As difficult as it is to imagine the mental and physical torture Jesus endured, it is certainly the spiritual weight of the world's sin and the suffering under God's divine wrath that is beyond human understanding. The only glimpses we have of the horror Jesus endured are in Matthew 27:46 and 50 where we read that twice He "cried out with a loud voice" and the curious detail in Matthew 27:46 that He cried out in Aramaic, His native language.[21]

Why do you suppose Jesus cried out in His native language?

There are only three occasions recorded in Scripture where Jesus spoke or cried out toward heaven from the Cross.[22]

Read Luke 23:34, 46 and Matthew 27:46. What consistent truth did Jesus cling to?

What can you learn from Jesus's example when you face difficulties?

Even in His darkest hour, Jesus never lost sight of His Father's love. Though Jesus experienced unimaginable torture and felt forsaken by God, His spirit clung to His Father ("My God!" and "Father!") until He could finally say, "It is finished" (John 19:30).

Our Hearts Cry Out, "Abba, Father!"

When I look back on the difficult story I shared at the beginning of yesterday's lesson, I am not surprised that one of the most painful wounds of rejection I experienced happened within the first few months of God opening my eyes to His love. I can just picture Satan sneering with delight. Not only because I suffered, but in the hopes that, because I was a baby Christian, the pain would draw me away from my heavenly Father. After all, Scripture tells us plainly that our enemy is not "flesh and blood," but "the spiritual forces of evil in the heavenly places" (Eph. 6:12).

The sad reality is that wounded people attract wounded people. As God calls me to share some difficult stories, I am ever mindful of my past dysfunctions that contributed to my unhealthy relationships and poor choices. Can you imagine if others only knew the worst moments of your life? What a distorted picture they would have. Just as my past failures, which are deep and many, do not define who I am, the events I share with you do not define the people who hurt me.[23] For years, I have prayed that they would receive the glorious gift Jesus offers to all who come to Him.

"Father, forgive them . . . "

Nevertheless, I did not realize how deeply the rejection of that dark night wounded my soul until many years later. It was my forty-eighth birthday. Although my friends and I had plans to celebrate that weekend, my birthday was on a Thursday, which is the day I typically set aside each week for my Sabbath rest (a date with Jesus). As was my habit, I spent the day at a quiet beach, praying, walking, journaling, and of course, resting. At one point, I sensed Jesus asking me to go deeper with Him, but I did not know how. I knew I was afraid and kept asking God to expose my fears and show me His love in a way I could understand.

That was when God exposed that old wound—a wound I had kept buried for nearly eighteen years. The wound was deep and painful. When God brought back the memory of that night, it was then that I decided He had gone too far. I felt angry—even betrayed—that He would cause me to re-experience such humiliation and heartache—that He would allow me feel so . . . broken. I could feel the anxiety swelling within me. It was the first time I ever accused God of anything. It just came out: raw, unadulterated emotion.

You don't understand, God! You may have come to earth as a human, but you did not come here as a woman!

Frenzied with tears, I continued, *You don't know what it's like to be a woman and treated like that: to give yourself over to someone only to be rejected and virtually spat upon.*

Suddenly, an image of Jesus on the Cross flashed in my mind. Having given all of Himself only to be rejected, beaten, spat on, and worse as the world shook its fists, hissing, *No thanks. We don't want you. We don't love you. You're not worth living for.*

My heart broke.

Then, right there in the darkness of my despair, I envisioned Jesus tenderly picking me up and carrying me in His arms. I wrapped my arms around His neck, not knowing—or caring—where He was taking me. Then I saw Jesus gently lay me in the arms of my heavenly Father. That's when I began to cry—out loud, right there on the beach. Clinging tightly to God as though I could somehow disappear in the safety of His love, I cried and cried, only able to voice one word: *Daddy*. For the next half hour or so, nothing else crossed my lips but a deep moaning . . . *Daddy . . . Daddy . . .*

Jesus knew that what I needed most in that dark hour was not a husband, or a counselor, or even a friend. I needed a daddy.

No matter what you or I endure in this life, Jesus understands. He knows our pain all too well. As He dropped to His knees in the garden, He cried out "Abba, Father" (Mark 14:36). Wracked with pain and torment on the Cross, He again cried out in His childhood language—no filter, just raw emotion of the Son crying out to His Father in heaven.

························Your Turn ·······························

How about you? When was the last time you envisioned yourself coming into God's presence as a little child?

How has this experience enriched your relationship with God?

If you have never experienced approaching God as a little child, ask God if there is anything holding you back from experiencing Him as a loving Father. If the words Father and Daddy are painful for you, be honest with God and give yourself permission to use another word, such as Papa or Abba, the Aramaic form for daddy, as spoken by Jesus Himself. Write what God reveals to you.

While we are to be always mindful to revere God, honoring His Holy Name, acknowledging His authority, and humbly bowing before Him, let us rejoice that through His Son Jesus Christ, we become children of God whereby we also come to know Him as Father—even *Daddy*.

Father in heaven, You are God and You are love—the true love that each of our hearts is desperately searching for. Open our eyes to Your love; open our hearts to Your peace and presence, which is only possible because of the price Jesus paid on the Cross to save us from ourselves, our rebellion, our helplessness, and our hopelessness.

"And because you are [His children], God has sent the Spirit of his Son into our hearts, crying, 'Abba! Father!" —Galatians 4:6

Witnessing God's Passion

Thank You, Jesus, for dying for our sins, for taking our sins in Your body, for suffering the punishment we deserve so we can shed the chains of guilt and lies that keep us in bondage to the enemy who seeks our misery and destruction. Thank You that You won the victory on the Cross. Give us the courage to run into Your arms. Help us to see the truth that Your love is safe, pure, and eternal—that everyone who comes to You with a fully surrendered heart can never be plucked out of Your hand. Amen.

Lesson Summary

What Scripture, statement, or thought was most significant to you this week? In the margin, write it down, and then reword it into a prayer of response to God.

There is a worship song that I truly enjoy, which beautifully captures the heart of this week's lesson. It is called "O, Come to the Altar" by Elevation Worship. Perhaps you will enjoy it as well.

Notes

[1] L. Morris, *The Gospel According to Matthew* (Grand Rapids, MI: Eerdmans, 1992), 512–13.

[2] In Romans 5:1–5, the word translated rejoice (*kau-[c]hao-mai*) literally means "to boast" (or glory, or exult).

[3] "Messiah" in *Baker Encyclopedia of the Bible* , ed. W. A. Elwell, (Grand Rapids, MI: Baker Book House, 1988), vol. 2, 1446.

[4] This is not to say that this is the first reference in the Bible to Jesus's identity as God's Son (see Luke 1:35), or the first use of the expression "son(s) of God" (such as is found in Job 1:6 concerning angels or in Luke 3:38 concerning Adam), but rather that this is the first occurrence in Scripture of the title "Son of God" being spoken directly to Jesus and, unlike references to angels or Adam, the title here signifies Jesus's deity.

[5] See also Matthew 28:18, 1 Timothy 6:15, and Revelation 17:14.

[6] Based on Matthew 2:7–18, it is unlikely that Satan knew Jesus's identity prior to Jesus's baptism. Only after God spoke from heaven, "This is my beloved Son," did Jesus begin his public ministry. Afterward, Scripture reveals that demons knew who Jesus was (Mark 1:34; Luke 4:41).

[7] Bruce A. Ware, *The Man Christ Jesus* (Wheaton, IL: Crossway, 2012), 84.

[8] T. Cabal et al., eds., *The Apologetics Study Bible* (Nashville: Holman Bible Publishers, 2007), 1826.

[9] However, there is no consensus among biblical scholars as to whether, in the midst of temptation, Jesus *knew* he was incapable of sin.

[10] Verse 5 of Matthew 21 is quoted from Zechariah 9:9.

[11] R. C. Sproul, *The Purpose of God: Ephesians* (Scotland, UK: Christian Focus Publications, 1994), 101–102.

[12] In traditional Jewish culture, women and men ate separately at meals. It would be reprehensible for a woman to interrupt a gathering of men. Even worse is daring to touch the men, as Mary boldly reached out and touched Jesus.

[13] Jesus rode into Jerusalem on a donkey on Sunday; the Last Supper and his subsequent arrest in the Garden of Gethsemane took place the following Thursday night/Friday morning.

[14] R. C. Sproul, *A Walk with God: An Exposition of Luke* (Scotland, UK: Christian Focus Publications, 1999), 395.

[15] In the Gospel of Matthew alone, Jesus addressed this in a number of passages, including 16:21; 17:22–23; 20:18–19; and 26:1–2.

[16] I. Howard Marshall, *The Gospel of Luke: A Commentary on the Greek Text* (Grand Rapids, MI: Eerdmans, 1978), 831.

[17] R. Hawker, *Poor Man's New Testament Commentary,* vol. 1, *Matthew–John* (Bellingham, WA: Logos Bible Software, 2013), 502–3.

[18] Whether or not the counsel I received at the time was fully in line with God's way is difficult to say; nonetheless, I believe it was offered in sincerity of heart.

[19] W. Smith, *Smith's Bible Dictionary* (Nashville: Thomas Nelson, 1986), Logos edition.

[20] Hawker, *Poor Man's New Testament*, 196.

[21] Jesus's words may be a combination of Hebrew and Aramaic, with "my God, my God" being a transliteration by Matthew from Hebrew. In Morris, *Gospel According to Matthew*, 720.

[22] Jesus spoke from the Cross to other persons (his mother and the disciple John, for example); however, the focus here is those times when Jesus spoke or cried out toward heaven.

[23] However, this is not to say that the events should be glossed over or the painful consequences marginalized.

PART IV

WEDDING

CELEBRATING GOD'S PURPOSE

CAN YOU BELIEVE WE ARE IN OUR FINAL WEEK? I CAN hardly wait for the days ahead when we will discover how Hagar's story foreshadows events she could never have imagined. Every story in the Bible has a purpose within God's grand design—and your story has a purpose as well. This week, as you retrace the steps of your own desert wanderings, you will find that your trials—just like Hagar's—serve a magnificent purpose: to draw you into the faithful arms of the "God Who Sees Me."

DAY ONE
Trusting in God's Purpose Right Where You Are

Hagar has come a long way: from the riches of Egypt, to a life of slavery, to a desert of despair. Then, just when all seemed lost, she heard a voice from heaven: "Rise!"

However, to help us fully grasp how Hagar's life, as well as yours and mine, fits into God's story, we first need to recognize what God's story is all about. The short answer is simply this: it's all about Jesus. From Genesis to Revelation, all of Scripture points to Him; He said so Himself (Luke 24:27).

Yet to His own brothers, the Israelites, Jesus looked nothing like what they expected. They expected their Messiah to want to be served. Instead, He washed

229

His disciples' feet. They expected a king to take back their nation by force. Instead, He refused to defend Himself when brought to trial. They expected Him to march in with the armies of heaven. Instead, He subjected Himself to a torturous and humiliating death. In every way, Jesus challenged the people's view of God.

He still does today.

PAUSE TO PONDER

Reflect back to when you first began this study. How has your view of God been challenged or expanded during this study?

Fear Not; God Is with You

Refresh your memory by rereading Genesis 16:10 and 17:20.

Have any of God's promises been fulfilled at this point?

Glance back through Genesis 21:8–21.

How many times is Ishmael mentioned by name?

What appears to be the author's focus in verses 15–21?

Reread Genesis 21:17b in the margin, taking note of the assurance that God heard Ishmael "where he is." Was Hagar and Ishmael's banishment from God's covenant community a banishment from God's presence? Explain.

"What troubles you, Hagar? Fear not, for God has heard the voice of the boy where he is."

—Genesis 21:17b

PAUSE TO PONDER

How can you take comfort in knowing there is no place that God does not hear your cry?

HOW DOES THE QURAN'S TEACHING OF HAGAR AND ISHMAEL COMPARE TO THAT OF THE BIBLE?

While an exhaustive study on the teaching of the Quran is outside the intent of this study, I did a bit of research and discovered a number of interesting contrasts.

The Bible	The Quran
GENERAL OVERVIEW	
Hagar is mentioned by name 16 times in Genesis (also twice in Paul's analogy in Galatians).	Hagar is never mentioned by name.
Ishmael is mentioned by name 24 times in the Old Testament:[1] 21 times in Genesis 3 times in 1 Chronicles 1	Ishmael is mentioned 12 times by name. (Sura 2:125, 127, 133, 136, 140; 3:84; 4:163; 6:86; 14:39; 19:54; 21:85; and 38:48)
Key events in the lives of Hagar and Ishmael include Hagar's encounters with God, as well as Ishmael's birth, death, children, grandchildren, and great-grandchildren, which span a total of 55 verses in the Bible across 7 chapters (Gen. 16:1–16; 17:18–20, 23, 25–26; 21:9–21; 25:9, 12–18; 28:9; 36:3–4, 10, 13, 17; 1 Chron. 1:28–31, 35, 37).	Ishmael is referenced in 17 verses. Of those, 7 relate to Abraham's dream of sacrificing Ishmael (Sura 37:102–105) or Abraham and Ishmael building a place of worship (Sura 2:125–127). Other references cite Ishmael as a prophet, (Sura 2:133, 2:136, 3:84, 4:163, 6:86), commend his character (Sura 19:54, 21:85, 38:48), or make a general reference (2:140, 14:39).
WHEN IT WAS WRITTEN	
Genesis was written around 1440 BC— approximately 80 years after the death of Ishmael.	The Quran was written sometime after 632 AD (the death of Muhammad)—approximately 2,070 years after the death of Ishmael.

Today, Ishmael is commonly recognized as the ancestor of the nomadic tribes of northern Arabia. Together with the sons of Keturah (whom Abraham married after the death of Sarah; Gen. 25:1–4), these comprise the majority of the modern Arabian nations. Islam did not surface until some 2,100 years after the life of Ishmael, when Muhammad began teaching the principles of the Quran.

The rise of Islam or any other false religion never takes God by surprise. God created time; He is not bound by it. As a matter of fact, God predicts these events in the Scriptures when Israel's enemies, including the Ishmaelites, boast, "Come, let us wipe them out as a nation; let the name of Israel be remembered no more!" (Ps. 83:4–6).

> If the eternal, all-knowing God wanted to prevent the birth of Ishmael, He could easily have done so . . . but He did not. God's love for Hagar, Ishmael, and all people created in His image is not in the least dependent on anything any of us has done or will do—whether good or bad. Rather, God's love for people is based on *who He is*. Because God is infinite, perfect, and unchanging, His infinite, perfect love for us is the same yesterday, today, and tomorrow and, through the Cross of Jesus Christ, is available to all who come to Him. As for me, being a descendant of Ishmael through my father, I am eternally grateful.
>
> "For God so loved the world, that he gave his only Son, that whoever believes in him should not perish but have eternal life" (John 3:16). And "there is no distinction between Jew and Greek; for the same Lord is Lord of all . . . For 'everyone who calls on the name of the Lord will be saved'" (Rom. 10:12–13; see also Amos 9:11–12 and Acts 15:13–19).

As far as we know, Ishmael's only knowledge of God up to this point would have come through stories he heard from his parents or others. Further, any experience he had of God would have been within the confines of his father's covenant community—the only life Ishmael had ever known. Then suddenly, everything changed. Would what Ishmael had come to believe about God in the security of his father's camp also be true in a lonely, hostile wilderness? Did banishment from his father Abraham's presence mean banishment from God Himself?

And what about Hagar? Had God forgotten His promise to bless her with descendants too numerous to count? Did the "God Who Sees Me" turn His face away? Never. There is no place too far, too dark, or too desperate that God is not there.

Our Hearts Cry Out, "Abba, Father!"

For many of us, it is easy to believe in God's goodness when life is going our way, but when we find ourselves feeling forsaken and abandoned, stripped of everything we hold dear, that is when our faith will be tested. Jesus knows our sorrow. Beaten, stripped, and hanging on a cross, He cried out "Father!" (Luke 23:46), echoing the heart-cry of every human soul: from the lowliest slave to the loftiest king.

God, do you see me?

Hagar may have felt entirely alone, but her tears never went unnoticed by *El Roi*. And what about Ishmael? Lying at death's door, feeling forsaken by his father and abandoned by his mother . . . *Father!* Surely this was the boy's heart-cry, perhaps not in words, but in sorrow of soul.

"Where shall I go from your Spirit? Or where shall I flee from your presence?"

—Psalm 139:7

God Meets Us Outside the Camp

Read Hebrews 13:12–14.

Where did Jesus suffer?

In what way was this similar to Hagar and Ishmael's situation?

Read the following passages; then answer the questions that follow.

John 8:34   Galatians 3:28–29; 4:6–7   Ephesians 2:1–2

Apart from Christ, how were we in slavery?

Who are included as Abraham's offspring?

> "And because you are [His children], God has sent the Spirit of his Son into our hearts, crying, 'Abba! Father!'" —Galatians 4:6

PAUSE TO PONDER

By becoming a child of God, what did you lose and what did you gain?

Take a few moments to write a prayer of thanksgiving to your "Abba, Father."

The Story Is Not Over

Although the events of Genesis 21 are the last words Scripture records directly about Hagar, her story is far from over, as we will soon discover. At the same time, while Ishmael is never mentioned by name, we are given a hint of events to come when we read, "God was with the boy." Then, beginning at Genesis 21:22 and continuing until Genesis 25, the story of Hagar and Ishmael moves into the background while the stories of Abraham, Sarah, and Isaac take center stage.

In Week Five, we journeyed with Abraham as he faced the ultimate test of faith on Mount Moriah (Gen. 22). For the purposes of this study, we will skip Genesis 23 and 24, which recount the death of Sarah followed by Abraham's arrangement of a wife for his son Isaac. We pick up the story of Hagar and Ishmael in Genesis 25.

Read Genesis 25:1-11; then answer the questions that follow. (Note: All of the names in Genesis 25:2 are masculine.[2])

How many sons did Abraham have all together?

List the names of the sons that came together to bury Abraham.

What conclusions can you make?

God Keeps His Promises

Many years have passed since Hagar and Ishmael were banished from Abraham's community. Ishmael is roughly ninety years old when his father Abraham dies. Apart from Isaac, Ishmael is the only other son Scripture records as returning to bury their father. It seems that during all those years, Ishmael never traveled so far as to remain out of reach. Given the bond between Abraham and Ishmael, as well as the Angel of the Lord's prophecy that Ishmael would live "to the east" (NASB) or "in the presence" (KJV) of all his brothers, this should not be surprising. Then, at the grave of the one who loved them both, the brothers are reunited[3]—a beautiful foreshadowing of God the Father reconciling His children to one another and Himself.

Read Genesis 25:12-18.

How many times is Ishmael mentioned by name?

What appears to be the author's focus in this passage?

List the names of each of Ishmael's sons.

Compare this passage with Genesis 16:10 and 17:20. How did God keep His promise?

PAUSE TO PONDER

Have you ever questioned God's commitment to you? Explain.

How does God's faithfulness to
Hagar encourage you personally?

How can you guard yourself
against doubting God's faithfulness?

Not only does Scripture confirm God's faithfulness to Hagar and blessing upon Ishmael, but there is something else in the narrative that is quite curious. The combination of expressions "breathed his last" and "gathered to his people" after a person dies is used of only four people in the entire Bible.[4] Let's take a look.

Read the verses listed in the following table.

In the second and third columns, record the name and age of the person who died.

In the last column, include a brief description of each person based on what you have learned. The description can include details such as their family lineage, key events from their lives, or facts surrounding their birth or death. I completed the first one to get you started.

	Name	Age upon Death	Brief Description
Genesis 25:7–8	Abraham	175	*Son of Terah; called by God to leave homeland; declared righteous by God; married to Sarah; promised descendants as numerous as the stars; father of Isaac and Ishmael; buried in a cave in the field of Ephron the Hittite*
Genesis 25:17			

Genesis 35:28-29			
Genesis 47:28; 49:29-33			

Does anything about this list surprise you? Share your thoughts. ⟡

Commentary author Dr. John Currid writes, "The three verbs, 'expired' [or 'breathed his last'], 'died' and 'gathered', were all applied to Abraham in 25:8. This is a formula used in Genesis for the deaths of famous Hebrew leaders. . . . Its use here in the case of Ishmael is unique, for he is not one of the promised seed or line."[5]

While it is true that Ishmael was not the promised child of God, much about his life was indeed unique. In Week Two, we learned that Ishmael is the first person named by God before he was born. He is also the first person mentioned as receiving the sign of God's covenant (Gen. 17:23). Not only did God promise to bless him, but He also promised to make Ishmael into a great nation (Gen. 17:20; 21:18). When Ishmael was torn from his home and father, we are assured that "God was with the boy" (Gen. 21:20). Finally, when Scripture records that Ishmael lived a long life (137 years!), "breathed his last," and "was gathered to his people," he is once again included in quite a distinguished group. From his birth to his death, the life of Hagar's son Ishmael was unique indeed.

But wait. What about Hagar? While it is true that there is no further mention of Hagar in the Bible, we will soon discover that her story echoes farther than she could ever have imagined. Even more, as we learned earlier in this study, Hagar is also linked to several key "firsts" in the Bible.

List all of the "firsts" you can recall about Hagar's life.

Which "first" do you find especially inspiring? Why? ⟡

In Week Two, we learned that Hagar was the first person to be met by the Angel of the Lord. She was also the first (and only) person to give God a name. As we just read, her child was the first person named by God before he was born. There are two other "firsts" that really touch my heart. When Hagar reached the end of herself, she was the first person in the Bible to watch helplessly as her only child lay dying. Then, from her desert of despair, she "lifted up her voice and wept"—the first mention of anyone weeping in Scripture.

Praise God this is not the end! There is good news! Hagar—a foreign-born female slave—is also the first person of whom Scripture says, "God opened her eyes," and as we discovered in Week Five, "Hagar becomes the first person . . . to undergo transformation in the wilderness leading to the founding of a wilderness nation."[6] Yet even here, Hagar's story is not over. Oh no, there is much more going on Behind the Seen. As a matter of fact, as we will discover tomorrow, Hagar's life foreshadows even greater events to come.

Your Turn

Where in your life at this time do you need to know God sees you right where you are?

Do you believe God has a purpose for you in this situation? Explain.

What if God's purposes were not revealed to you in this life? Would you still trust His plan? Share your thoughts.

Is there a "Hagar" or "Ishmael" in your life—someone who needs to know God sees and loves them right where they are? Ask God to help you see this person through His eyes and then invite Him to show you what you can do to offer encouragement to this person. Commit what He reveals to you in the margin.

DAY TWO
Seeing Your Story Redeemed for God's Purposes

What part of our study of Hagar has been most memorable to you? If a friend asked you what you learned from the study, what would you say?

Celebrating God's Purpose

At the introduction to this study, I remarked on how little many of us know about the story of Hagar as compared to some of the more famous Bible characters, such as Noah, Abraham, and Moses.

Without looking at any resources, list everything you remember having read or heard about Moses.

Look over the list you just wrote. Do you notice any parallels between the lives of Hagar and Moses? If so, write them down.

The Bigger Picture

The table lists several key facts about Hagar's life. Fill in each blank using one of the following words or phrases. (For a review of Hagar's story, glance back at Genesis 16:1, 6–7, 9–13).

angel   sent   threatened   Egypt   name   the wilderness
slavery   wealthy   ran away   spring of water

Hagar's Story
Born in _____
A slave
Grew up with a _____ family
Felt _____ by someone in the family and _____
After running away, stopped at a _____
Met an _____ of the Lord in _____
God acknowledged the affliction of _____
God was given a _____
God _____ her back to the place she left

We will now read a brief overview of Moses's story. Please read the following passages in the book of Exodus:

1:1–5   2:1–2   2:10–15   3:1–2, 7–14   15:22–25

Listed in the table are the aspects of Hagar's story you reviewed previously. Place an X in the center column next to each circumstance if it also appears in Moses's story.

	True for Moses's story	True for Hagar's story
Born in Egypt		X
A slave (or born a slave)		X
Grew up with a wealthy family		X
Felt threatened by someone in the family and ran away		X
After running away, stopped by a well (or spring) of water		X
Met the Angel of the Lord in the wilderness		X
God acknowledged affliction of slavery		X
God was given a Name or gave His Name		X
God sent him (her) back to the place he (she) left		X

Ponder the table for a few moments. Did anything surprise you? Share your thoughts. *Off*

I love the fact that while the story of Moses leading the Israelites is central to God's redemptive story, He first reveals Himself to a lowly Egyptian runaway slave, promising to "multiply your offspring so that they cannot be numbered for multitude" (Gen. 16:10). Through Hagar's story and countless others, Scripture is unfolding for us God's redemptive plan for all the nations of the earth. God demonstrates His intimate love and concern for individuals, without regard for race, nationality, gender, social status, or anything else. God is infinite. His love has no bounds. God is no less concerned about Hagar's affliction than He is for His entire beloved people of Israel. As a matter of fact, Hagar's affliction foreshadows Israel's own, as we are about to discover.

Compare and contrast Genesis 16:7, 10-11 with Exodus 3:1-2, 7-8. What parallels can you discover?

"Worthy are you to take the scroll and to open its seals, for you were slain, and by your blood you ransomed people for God from every tribe and language and people and nation, and you have made them a kingdom and priests to our God, and they shall reign on the earth."
—Revelation 5:9-10

From Slavery to Royalty

The similarities that mark key events in Hagar and Moses's lives are quite remarkable, yet they have even more than this in common. Both Hagar and Moses wrestled with the unique challenge of having dual identities. Although Hagar was a slave, her mistress Sarah temporarily positioned Hagar as Abraham's surrogate wife. Although Moses was born a slave, when Pharaoh's daughter adopted him, he temporarily became a prince of Egypt. From slavery to royalty: the stuff dreams and fairy tales are made of. However, in both cases, their elevated positions would not last. It was simply not in accordance with God's purposes, which were far greater than either of them could ever have imagined.

> Compare and contrast Genesis 21:15-20 and Exodus 15:22-25. (Note: "Marah" refers to a spring of water in the wilderness of Shur; it is the first place the people of Israel camped after crossing the Red Sea.)
>
> Summarize all the parallels you can discover in these passages.

Just as God met Hagar in the wilderness, acknowledged her affliction, and comforted her with a promise, God met Moses in the wilderness, acknowledged the affliction of His people, and promised deliverance.

And just as God freed Hagar from slavery, sent her back into the wilderness, saved her son from dying of thirst, and then called Hagar to participate in His plan to raise up Ishmael into "a great nation," God used Moses to free the Israelites from slavery, sent them into the wilderness, and saved them from dying of thirst, and as a result, a wilderness nation was born. In all of these scenarios, it was in the wilderness, when all appeared lost, that each experienced God's presence, power, and provision.

> It is often in the wilderness, when all appears lost, that we experience God's presence, power, and provision.

PAUSE TO PONDER

Why do you think God chose the wilderness
as the place where He revealed Himself:

To Hagar and Ishmael?

To Moses and the Israelites?

How does seeing Hagar's story in light of
Moses's story speak to you personally?

Seeing Your Story with New Eyes

Throughout our lives, each of us will experience both trials and blessings. Very often, we later discover that they were actually two sides of the same coin. During this study, you have paused to reflect on how God has used trials ("wilderness years") in your own life to accomplish something good. We're now going to bring these together to see if we can discover the bigger picture Behind the Seen.

In earlier weeks, you completed six fill-in questions (pages 30, 45, 62, 93, 151, 181). Using your previous responses to these questions, complete the timeline exercises that follow. (Note: As an example, I have included a timeline of my own at the end of these instructions.)

Blessings

But God	But God	But God	But God	But God	But God

Year born   Your age today

Trials

On the timeline, write the year you were born at the far left and your current age at the far right. Next, look back at each of the six questions listed from prior weeks. Then do the following.

Plot the approximate age (or age range) you were at the time of each trial.

Underneath each age you entered on the timeline, briefly describe the trial you faced at that time.

Finally, write the corresponding blessing you later experienced in the space above your description of the trial. (Suggestion: Begin each blessing with the words, "But God...")

Listed below are some examples of how God may have used difficult circumstances for good. Perhaps, as you reviewed the fill-in questions from earlier weeks, there are one or more situations for which you struggle to recognize how God used it for good. If that is the case, take a few moments to ponder the examples in the following list. Spend some time in prayer asking God to reveal how He was at work in your situation. Then go back and complete your timeline as God enables you.

God renewed my (passion for ministry, sense of self-worth)
God strengthened my (faith, resolve, commitment, character)
God brought restoration to my (relationships, heart, body)
God birthed a passion for ministry to (orphans, prisoners, single moms)
God taught me (perseverance, patience, obedience)
God increased my (compassion, mercy, humility)

If different trials and corresponding blessings come to mind, feel free to include those on your timeline as well.

The following timeline includes some of the trials and blessings from my own life.

Blessings

But God birthed a ministry to post-abortive women	But God taught me how to forgive	But God brought new friends whom He used to introduce me to Himself!	But God taught me true intimacy and healed me of co-dependency and other dysfunctions	But God opened the door for me to go to seminary
age 15	age 17	age 30 †	age 31	age 43
I had an abortion	I was drugged and raped	Work required my spouse and I to leave home and move across country	My marriage ended in divorce	I lost a job I thoroughly enjoyed

Year born: 1967

Your age today: age 50

Trials

Next, place a cross on your timeline based on the age you were when Jesus became your Lord and Savior. If you have not received God's gift of salvation through Jesus Christ, perhaps now is the time to do so. "I tell you that the 'right time' is now, and the 'day of salvation' is now" (2 Cor. 6:2 NCV).

Sometimes we think God cannot use us because of our past, but that is a lie straight from the enemy. Remember the woman at the well, about whom we studied in Week Two? Of all people, Jesus chose an adulterous woman of Samaria as the first person to whom He would reveal Himself as the Messiah. As a result, God transformed an isolated outcast into a courageous witness of God's grace who brought the Good News to her entire village!

And what about Hagar? A used and abused runaway pagan slave? *This* is God's choice to whom He reveals Himself as *El Roi*, the "God Who Sees Me"? Yes, for God does not see as man sees. He looks past race, reputation, nationality, gender, social status. . . . He looks upon the one thing that truly matters: the heart (1 Sam. 16:7). For reasons we may not fully realize on this side of heaven, it is often out of our deserts of despair that, if our hearts are willing, God will dig the deepest wells overflowing with living water.

Each of us, with all of our triumphs and failures, joys and heartbreaks, scars and all, has been given an opportunity to make a difference in our world. Never underestimate what God can do with a life solely surrendered to Him. Just as God had His eye on Hagar, He has His eye on you. Give God your "wilderness years," for who knows if they have been preparing you "for such a time as this."[7]

······························Your Turn······························

How has God used the "wilderness years" of your life to open your eyes to His presence? What impact have these seasons had on your relationship with God?

Take some extended time this week to reflect upon your timeline. In what way(s) do you see God redeeming your story for His purposes? How is God using your experiences to minister to or be a witness to others? Be prepared to discuss with your group.

As best as you are able, write a prayer of thanksgiving for the "wilderness years."

> "Come, everyone who thirsts come to the waters; and he who has no money, come, buy and eat! Come, buy wine and milk without money and without price."
> —Isaiah 55:1

> "As for you, you meant evil against me, but God meant it for good."
> —Genesis 50:20

Today's lesson required a lot of heart work. A tender worship song that you may enjoy is "Sovereign Over Us" by Aaron Keyes.

DAY THREE
Rising Up to Embrace God's Call

I will never forget the night . . .

It was April 3, 2015. Good Friday. I was home alone watching the movie *Passion of the Christ*. With tears streaming down my face as I watched the horror of the crucifixion, my heart cried out, *Oh Jesus, why!?! Why would you do that for us? Why would you do that for me? What, oh Lord, did you see?!? What did you see that could possibly hold you there?*

"I saw you."

For the Joy Set before Him

I have never forgotten those words.

His words still echo today. No matter what we have done or how we have suffered, Jesus's blood still testifies, *I want you. I love you. You are worth fighting for. You are worth dying for.*

PAUSE TO PONDER

> Write your name in front of each of the following sentences. Imagine that Jesus is speaking to you, and then read each sentence slowly and out loud.
>
> _____, I see you.
>
> _____, I want you.
>
> _____, I love you.
>
> _____, you are worth fighting for.
>
> _____, you are worth dying for.
>
> Which truth stirs your heart the most? Why?
>
> Ask God if there is anything in the way of you living wholeheartedly in light of these truths. Write down what He reveals to you.

Even in His darkest hour, Jesus could have ended it all, but He did not. Why? "I saw you."

Sidebar quotes:

"You are the God who sees me." —Genesis 16:13 NIV

". . . for the joy set before Him, He endured the cross . . ." —Hebrews 12:2 NIV

Hebrews 12:2 tells us, "For the joy set before Him, He endured the cross. . . ." Joy. He did it for the joy that was waiting for Him on the other side: the joy of seeing you and me and all of God's children from every tribe, nation, and tongue reconciled to God the Father, to Himself, and to one another.

The Mystery of Victory

In Colossians 1:16, the apostle Paul tells us that everything in all creation was made by, for, and through Jesus Christ, and that He holds all things together. Therefore, no circumstances have entered into our lives that have not been allowed by God. He created mankind with dignity to make its own choices. At the same time, God is holy and grieves every injustice.

Because we live in a fallen world, like Hagar, you and I may experience many dark days, but if we will trust our heavenly Father and surrender to His perfect plan, He will often use our darkest days to shine forth His glorious light.

Let us look at a great example from the Gospel of John.

Read John 9:1–7.

According to Jesus, why was the man born blind?

Consider the text carefully. Which came first: the man's suffering or God's plan to relieve his suffering?

Was it necessary for the man to understand his circumstances in order to be a part of God's plan?

How can this truth strengthen and encourage you when you experience suffering or difficult circumstances?

Freedom rarely comes in the way we expect. For the blind man, freedom from suffering came alongside a realization that being born blind was actually part of God's plan. For Hagar, freedom did not come with an elevated social status (temporary or otherwise), but rather it came after being abandoned into a barren wilderness.

Glance back at Genesis 21:17–19.

Which happened first: God's call for Hagar to rise up, or God opening her eyes?

> Then the Lord said to him, "Who has made man's mouth? Who makes him mute, or deaf, or seeing, or blind? Is it not I, the Lord?"
> —Exodus 4:11

What significance might this have? ❦

I love the fact that the one who gasped, "You are a God who sees me!" is the first person of whom Scripture testifies, "God opened her eyes." It was in the wilderness where Hagar gained her freedom and experienced God's presence, provision, and protection. It was there, after her hands were emptied of everything else—even her hopes and dreams—that she was finally free to embrace God's call, "Up! Lift up the boy with your hand. . . ."

As if God was saying, *Now you are ready to take hold of the plan I Myself have been preparing for you all along.*

The Call of God

Read the following passages. Pay special attention to the dialogue and record any common themes you can discover (the first passage is a review).

Genesis 21:17-18   Matthew 9:2-6   Matthew 26:32, 46
Luke 7:11-15   Luke 8:40-42, 49-55

God sees Behind the Seen. He saw Hagar and Ishmael's future. He saw the paralytic's faith. He demonstrated the hope of the resurrection . . . and all the scenes had one thing in common. Let's take a closer look.

In Genesis 21:18, after the Angel of God comforts Hagar, he gives her a command. The ESV translates it this way, "Up! Lift up the boy, and hold him fast with your hand. . . . " The Hebrew verb translated "Up!" is *qumi*, which means to arise or stand up. In Matthew 9:6, the command spoken by Jesus to the paralytic is *egertheis*, which means arise, stand up, or awaken. In Luke 7:13–14, after Jesus comforts the grieving widow whose only son had died, Jesus issues this same command to the dead man: "Arise!" And again in Luke 8:54, Jesus commands the deceased child, "Arise!" Finally, moments before His arrest, Jesus commands His sleepy disciples, "Rise!"—the exact same verb He uses in Matthew 26:32 to foretell His resurrection soon to come.

Hagar, rise! Young man, rise! Child, rise!

It's not over!

Beloved, it's not over! Right where you are, God is calling to you: *rise!*

In every scenario, the situation looked hopeless. Hagar's son was dying, the man was paralyzed, the child was dead, and the King of Glory was about to be arrested, tried, and killed. But God looks down from heaven and sees Behind the Seen. He sees what no one else could believe: *they . . . will . . . rise!*

Read Matthew 27:50-54 (verse 50 is a review).

What happens within moments of Jesus's death?

What happens after Jesus is raised from the dead? Be specific.

What might the author be trying to demonstrate here?

Only Matthew's Gospel records the tombs breaking open and saints rising from the grave after Jesus's resurrection. Just as during Jesus's earthly life, the healings and other miraculous signs demonstrated Jesus was who He claimed to be, His resurrection from the dead and that of His saints demonstrated His ultimate victory over sin and the grave.

Even in death, the story is not over! The fact that only saints are mentioned is very significant. While on earth, Jesus healed both the grateful and the ungrateful (Luke 17:11–19). Each of them eventually died and entered eternity, but only those who belong to Christ will rise to live with Him forever.

Raised and Seated with Christ

Read Ephesians 2:4-6. List every truth that is yours in Jesus Christ.

Take a few moments to ponder these truths. Which one do you need to be reminded of today? Explain.

The verbs "raised" and "seated" in verse 6 are presented in Greek as a statement of fact.[8] Because God exists outside of time, to Him we are already raised and seated with Christ in the heavenly places, and nothing in all creation can change this truth. This is the foundation of our Christian hope! Our hope of heaven is not wishful thinking or fairy tales, but a fixed, eternal fact.

Rise! "It is finished" (John 19:30).

Praise the Lord! Jesus Christ has won the victory! The Cross demonstrates His great love for us. His resurrection reveals His power over death and the grave. He did it all so that we could become children of God, holy and beloved in His sight.

"I saw you."

································Your Turn································

Just as God called out to Hagar, He calls out to us. Just as God empowered Hagar to rise above her circumstances, He empowers us.

> Describe what it would look like to live in the full assurance and continuous awareness of being raised and seated with Christ. What impact would it have on:
>
> Your relationship with God?
>
> Your outlook on this life?
>
> Your witness for Christ?
>
> Ask God what steps you need to take to further anchor these truths in your life. Commit these steps in the form of a written prayer.

DAY FOUR
Setting Your Hope on the Kingdom

When I fell in love with Jesus, I believed He could return at any moment (I still do). Filled with a sense of urgency and my budding faith, I shared the story of Jesus with almost everyone I came into contact with. My family . . . my coworkers . . . I actually felt sorry for anyone seated next to me on an airplane. While some people responded receptively, most often my efforts left me in despair. Although I have since learned to be more sensitive to the individual needs of the other person, my favorite Bible verse from those days until now remains the same: "Those who go out weeping, carrying seed to sow, will return with songs of joy, carrying sheaves with them" (Ps. 126:6 NIV).

Formed and Fashioned for God's Purposes

As God begins to open our eyes to His call on each of our lives, we must never set our hope on destinations in this life, such as the fulfillment of our assignments. Our hope and joy lie far beyond any earthly "promised land." Except for the cave he was buried in, Abraham never owned a foot of ground of the land God promised him. Moses was not even permitted to set one sandal on the Promised Land but only saw it from a distance (Deut. 34:1–5). Then there is Hagar. We do not even know whether she lived to see God's promises concerning her son fulfilled. Still, what greater joy in this life could there be than to have experienced a personal encounter with the "God Who Sees Me"?

For each of them, it was the desert road—the detours, the struggles, the heart-aches and tears—not the destination that formed and fashioned them for God's great purposes. It is the same for each of us. When I look back on my own life, I can see many heartbreaks: I had an abortion, I was slipped the date-rape drug, my marriage suffered many dysfunctions and ultimately ended in divorce, and the list goes on. But God sees past our brokenness and our most severe disability of all—that is, our sin—to gaze upon who He created us to be: His beloved sons and daughters. And as God's children—rescued, redeemed, and restored—we bring Him glory and great joy by shining His glorious light into a dark and desolate world.

> It is the desert road—the detours, the struggles, the heartaches and tears—not the destination that forms and fashions us for God's great purposes.

PAUSE TO PONDER

Think back on this past week. List the top two or three things that occupied the majority of your thought life. Be specific.

Our Hope of Heaven

Read at least three of the following passages. Next to each one, record what it teaches about the Christian's hope.

Luke 2:9-11

John 16:16, 20-22

Ephesians 1:13–14

Philippians 3:20–21

1 Thessalonians 4:14–18

1 Peter 1:3–7

1 Peter 2:9–10

Of the passages you read, which one encourages you the most? Why?

The Kingdom Is at Hand

The Christian life means having a restored relationship to God the Father through His Son Jesus Christ. This relationship includes both a "here and already" aspect (something we can experience on earth right now), as well as a "there and not yet" aspect (something we will experience in heaven in the future).

Very often, we perceive heaven, or the kingdom of God, as a future experience and distant place, but it is so much more. In Luke 17:20–21, Jesus said to His disciples, "The kingdom of God is not coming in ways that can be observed . . . for behold, the kingdom of God is in the midst of you."

What does Jesus seem to be teaching in these verses?

To be in the kingdom of God is to be in relationship with God the Father through Jesus Christ. That relationship is not bound by time and space. It begins the moment Jesus enters your heart as Lord and Savior and continues for all eternity. To be knitted to Jesus is to be knitted to His Father's heart as well. However, as long as we remain in our earthly bodies, we exist simultaneously within two realms. Spiritually, we are already "raised and seated" with Christ in His holy heaven. Physically, we remain bound on this sin-cursed earth until the day Jesus will raise us and "transform our lowly body to be like his glorious body" (Phil. 3:21). Then, being clothed with purity, God the Father will present us to Jesus His Son as His beloved Bride. Together, we will live with Him in our heavenly home—on a new earth where righteousness reigns—for all eternity (Rev. 19:6–9; 21:1–3).

And that's no fairy tale!

"Who is that coming up

from the wilderness,

leaning on her beloved?"

—Song of Solomon 8:5

PAUSE TO PONDER

Read Revelation 21:1–5 and 22:1–5. What about
your eternal home do you long for the most?

An Eternal View

One day, Jesus will make all things new, death will be no more, and we will dwell
with the Lord where righteousness reigns forever (Ps. 45:6–7; Rev. 21:1–5). Yet as
wonderful as heaven will be, we need to be mindful that for a short time, for purposes only fathomable within the omniscient, holy mind of God, we still live in
enemy territory. The distractions and cares of this world will contend relentlessly
to gain our affections. With so many things vying for our attention in the here and
now, it can be challenging for us to keep our eyes fixed on that which is unseen.
That is why we must be intentional in what we allow to occupy our thoughts.

Our choices are driven by our thoughts. Our thoughts are driven by what
occupies our hearts. And that which occupies our hearts is where we have placed
our hope. If our hearts are centered on the hope of Christ and His kingdom, our
thoughts, cares, and choices will naturally follow. "For where your treasure is,
there your heart will be also" (Matt. 6:21).

One way to fan into flame our hope of heaven is to first step back and examine
our lives within the context of eternity.

Read the following verses. How can these passages help you keep your life
in perspective?

Psalm 8:3–4

Psalm 39:4–5

Psalm 90:1–6, 12

*If our hearts are centered
on the hope of Christ and
His kingdom, our thoughts,
cares, and choices will
naturally follow.*

When you and I imagine how our lives fit within eternity, we cannot help but
see how fleeting our lives are. At the same time, the fact that our heavenly Father
is intimately involved in the details of our lives should stir our hearts toward Him
in absolute adoration. This is why Hagar was astonished to discover that "You Are
a God Who Sees Me." The reason for pondering these truths is not to diminish
our view of our lives, but to explode our view of God!

The glorious reality of God's great purpose is unimaginably magnified by the fact that He would even care for us. In awe the psalmist asks, "What is man that you are mindful of him, and the son of man that you care for him?" (Ps. 8:4).

How can looking at your life in light of eternity help to develop a "kingdom mind-set"?

He Is Preparing a Place for Us

As a loving Father, God cares for us intimately. We are His precious children, but we are more than that. He is also preparing us to be the cherished Bride of His beloved Son.

In Jewish culture during biblical times, it was customary for a bridegroom who was pledged to be married to first return home and build a room onto his father's house where he and his bride would live. Once everything was ready, the bridegroom would return to his bride's hometown with great festivities, blowing a trumpet (a *shofar*, or ram's horn) announcing his arrival.

Read John 14:2–3 and Ephesians 1:3–4.

What is your bridegroom occupied with until He returns?

How long has He been at this task?

How long have you been on His mind?

What does this mean to you personally?

Read Revelation 22:7, 12–13, 20.

What does Jesus promise to do?

How many times did He repeat this promise?

What does this mean to you personally?

································Your Turn································

At the beginning of today's lesson, I asked you to write down the top two or three things that occupied the majority of your thought life this week. You may be dealing with very serious matters, or perhaps you wrestled to keep a dozen competing thoughts at bay, with few deserving much of your time. No matter where you are, or what you are dealing with, time is precious . . . and it is short. Your bridegroom is coming soon.

Read Matthew 6:25, 30-33.

Spend some time reflecting on your life in light of eternity. Is there anything you need to change? Explain.

What one or two specific steps will you take over the next week? Commit them to God through prayer. Write down your prayer.

DAY FIVE
Celebrating Your Victory in Christ

At the beginning of this study, I invited you to ponder with me:

Am I known? Am I loved? Am I home?

Every human heart is searching for the answers to these questions. Yet when pain and heartache enter our lives, we feel betrayed and cry out one question: *God, do you see me?*

The answer is yes. He is right here. Right now. Working on your behalf . . . Behind the Seen.

Celebrating God's Purpose

PAUSE TO PONDER

> As we reach the end of Hagar's story and our study, how have you been impacted personally by encountering *El Roi* through the Scriptures?

"...he has put eternity into man's heart."
—Ecclesiastes 3:11

Our Citizenship Is in Heaven

"You mean the brown house?"

I was on my cell phone chatting with my three-year-old niece who lives three thousand miles away. Just before saying good-bye, I asked her what I thought was a simple question: "What are you going to do when you get home?"

She replied, "You mean the brown house?"

I felt as if my heart broke into a thousand pieces. Her parents had just separated, and I had forgotten that the children were being shuffled back and forth between their parents' houses. My eyes welled with tears as I realized my sweet little niece no longer knew what it meant to be home.

Scripture teaches that every human heart longs for an eternal home. Many people go through life never recognizing the source of their restlessness; even so, it is always there. Saint Augustine, who lived over sixteen hundred years ago, captured this truth beautifully when he wrote, "Thou hast made us for thyself, O Lord, and our heart is restless until it finds its rest in thee."[9]

Compare Philippians 3:20 with Acts 20:24. What gave the apostle Paul the courage to live a life fully abandoned to God?

"Thou hast made us for thyself, O Lord, and our heart is restless until it finds its rest in thee."
—Saint Augustine, *Confessions*

Read Hebrews 11:1–2, 13–16. In what did these faithful saints place their hope?

Read Hebrews 12:1–2. Contrast a person who simply runs a race with one who runs with endurance.

As citizens of heaven, our hope is not in this life. Our hope lies beyond this life. Nevertheless, for a short time we still live in a foreign land, in enemy territory, but we need not fear, for our King has defeated the enemy—even the grave!

PAUSE TO PONDER

> What does it mean to you that your citizenship is in heaven?
>
> What would it look like for you to live your life fully abandoned to God? Is there something you need to cast aside? Explain.

We Are Christ's Beloved Bride

Not only does every human being long for an eternal home, but we also long to be loved. Scripture teaches that those who belong to Christ are also His Bride (Rev. 19:7–8). What a precious thought! As Christ's Bride, we are cherished beyond our wildest imagination. We are His Beloved (Song of Sol. 7:10), the one He shed His own blood for (Eph. 5:29–32). One day soon, He will take us home to be with Him forever. In the meantime, there is work to be done. Just as our bridegroom is in heaven preparing a place for us, we as His Bride are also getting ready for Him here on earth.

Rather than imagery of a bride's external adornment, such as clothing or jewelry,[10] Scripture describes believers as being Christ's own body, which He is "building up" into a holy temple (Matt. 16:18; Eph. 1:22–23; 2:21–22). But what does this mean exactly? One way to appreciate it is to look at the first time Scripture records God building something.

Read Genesis 2:18–25.

List everything God did.

What is the author's conclusion according to verse 24?

Let us explore these verses a bit deeper by examining a few of the words in Hebrew. (It will be worth it, I promise.) The word commonly translated "rib" in Genesis 2:22 is *sela*. It is actually an architectural term meaning side, side room, or supporting beam. The word is used repeatedly in Exodus 25 through 38 to refer to the assembly of the Tabernacle and again in Ezekiel 41 in reference to the construction of the Temple.

The Hebrew verb commonly translated "made"[11] in Genesis 2:22 is taken from the root word *banah*, which is also an architectural term, meaning "to build." This word should be familiar. It is the same word we studied in Week One when we read in Genesis 16:2 that Sarah sought to "build" a family.

Lastly, the word "naked" in Genesis 2:25 comes from the Hebrew root word *arom* and includes the idea of having no barrier.[12] Adam and Eve were "naked and not ashamed." There was no barrier between them and God or each other. Please keep these definitions in mind as we look at several passages in the New Testament.

> Compare and contrast the following passages. What similarities can you discover?
>
> John 19:30–34 with Genesis 2:21

> Ephesians 5:29–32 with Genesis 2:23–24

What additional insights can you glean from the following verses?

Mark 15:37–38   Ephesians 2:13–22   Hebrews 10:19–22

"As the bridegroom rejoices over the bride, so shall your God rejoice over you." —Isaiah 62:5

"Rejoice that your names are written in heaven." —Luke 10:20

PAUSE TO PONDER

How do these Scriptures contribute to your understanding of how Jesus sees you as His beloved Bride?

Your Names Are Written in Heaven

Each of us longs to be home, to be loved, and to be known. Because all of humanity is created in the image of God (Gen. 1:27), His church includes servant-heroes of all shapes and sizes, from all times and places, male and female, Jew and Gentile, slave and free (Gal. 3:28). While you and I will never know most of these saints this side of heaven, God knows every one of His servants by name (Luke 10:20 and Rev. 3:5).

Listed are several Scripture references. Read both passages from Isaiah as well as at least one passage from the New Testament. How do these verses contribute to your understanding of God's heart for all people?

Isaiah 56:6-7   Isaiah 60:3-7   Matthew 28:18-20   Romans 10:12-13
Galatians 3:28-29   Revelation 5:9

Isaiah 60:3-7 describes events relating to the eternal kingdom of God.[13] Do you recognize the names in verse 7? If not, glance back at Genesis 25:13. Describe where these names originate and what the prophet Isaiah writes about them.

Scripture assures us that through Christ's blood, God's eternal kingdom will include people ransomed "from every tribe and language and people and nation" (Rev. 5:9). How precious that God made it a point to record the descendants' names of our beloved heroine Hagar!

Yet, like Hagar, you and I may not witness the fulfillment of God's promises in this life. After Hagar provided a wife for her son, Scripture offers no clues as to what happened to her after that. Did she live to see her grandchildren? Did she marry? Did she witness Ishmael rise up into a great nation? Like so many heroes of the faith, Hagar may never have seen God's promises fulfilled in this life; nevertheless, God always keeps His promises.

The Mystery of the Gospel

In the apostle Paul's letter to the Ephesians, he describes the mystery of the gospel as the inclusion of Gentiles (Eph. 3:3–6). The word "mystery" is *mysterion* in Greek and stems from the Greek word *muo*, which means to shut the eyes (or mouth). In reality, this "mystery" was recorded throughout the Old Testament, beginning with God's promise to Abraham in Genesis 12:3.

Roughly 1,400 years after the life of Hagar, Ezekiel, a prophet and priest, had been exiled along with many Judeans to Babylon. There, God gave him visions of the future messianic kingdom, many of which are paralleled in the Book of Revelation.[14] In these visions, Ezekiel sees the future temple of God and divisions of the land, but there is something specific I want you to see for yourself.

Read Ezekiel 47:21-23. What promises are revealed in this passage?

We may never see God's promises fulfilled in this life; nevertheless, God always keeps His promises.

Reread Genesis 21:10-12. Compare this passage with Ephesians 3:6 and Ezekiel 47:21-23. What conclusions can you draw?

The passage in Ezekiel, as well as Exodus 12:48–49, Leviticus 19:34, and many other Old Testament verses, including those quoted in Romans 15:9–12, all point to God's heart for people of every tribe, nation, and tongue. However, even Paul, a Torah scholar and expert in Jewish Law, was blind to the "mystery" until God opened his eyes to the truth that had been there all along.

The Last Enemy

Read the following three verses. List every assurance conveyed.

Matthew 16:18

1 Corinthians 15:26

Revelation 1:18

Read Genesis 22:17 and Galatians 3:16.

Who does the seed (or offspring) of Abraham ultimately point to?

In addition to multiplying Abraham's offspring, what specific promise did God make concerning Abraham's seed?

How did God fulfill His promise to Abraham?

More Than Conquerors

Read Romans 8:28, 31–39; then fill in the blanks next to each question.

Question	Answer
What things work together for the good of those who love God?	
Who is for us?	
What did God give up for us?	
Who is interceding for us?	
What can separate you from the love of God?	
What are we called, *in spite of our trials*?	

If the "God Who Sees Me" can turn a pagan runaway into a servant of God and an exiled slave into the mother of a mighty nation, how much more will God use your life as a testimony of His power and glory? Beloved, there is no One more invested in your victory than the One who paid for it with His own blood. Let us ask Him, therefore, for the courage to believe we are "more than conquerors through him who loved us."

............................Your Turn ....

In the introduction to this study, you were asked, "Is the enemy using anything in your past to try to derail you from God's plan, or hold you back from experiencing God's joy to the fullest? Be assured, that is not how your story will end. Just as God did for Hagar, when He enters your story, victory is already assured."

How has the enemy been trying to derail you from God's plan, or hold you back from experiencing God's joy to the fullest? (Note: In Scripture, internal joy is often coupled with external hardships. See 1 Thess. 1:6; Heb. 10:32–34, 12:2.)

Which truth from Romans 8 can you apply in your circumstance?

What would it look like for you to be "more than a conqueror" in this situation? Be specific.

Interesting fact: The phrase "more than conquerors" is one word in Greek, *hypernikomen*, combining the word *hyper* (meaning "beyond") with *conquer*. In effect, through Christ, we are super-conquerors far beyond what it means to conquer in the physical realm.

Write a prayer of faith in response to what God reveals to you.

Lesson Summary

What Scripture, statement, or thought was most significant to you this week?
Write it down and then reword it into a prayer of response in the margin.

Beloved, I do not know what wilderness God has brought you through or what desert you may be walking in right now, but one thing I do know: our glorious King will not waste one tear, one cry, nor one anguished prayer. He sees each one and will use them for His glory in ways no one but He can conceive.

God, do you see me?

Oh yes, dear one. He sees you. Just like our heroine, you have journeyed from slavery to freedom, from betrayed to God's beloved, and from desert wandering to the hope of a heavenly dwelling. What the devil thought was your destruction has become your deliverance! In the same way that God did not merely free Hagar *from* something, but *for* something, you also have been set free for a purpose. Jesus declares, "You will be my witnesses. . . . Go therefore and make disciples of all nations . . ." (Acts 1:8, Matthew 28:19 selected).

Before we close, I would like to share a word with you from my private journal. The page is dated February 18, 2016. I remember the day. It was bright but chilly at the beach—my favorite spot for a weekly "date with Jesus." I was walking along the shore when I paused to gaze out over a patch of beautiful clouds. Right then, God prompted me to imagine speaking to the clouds as if they were people. "What would you say to them?" God asked. The words came quickly and effortlessly; I knew exactly what I would say. (It's so easy to be courageous in our thoughts, isn't it?) After I wrote in my journal what I would say, God rattled me with this pronouncement: "These words are for you." In that instant, I was humbled, amazed, and convicted all at the same time. These are the words I wrote, which God used to speak back to me—words that I believe reflect His heart for all who belong to Him.

Beloved, you are here on this speck of dust called earth, in this moment of time called today, with breath in your mouth and My Word in your heart to declare My glory in a lost, dying, and broken world. You did not arrive here by accident—neither at your conception nor in this very moment—you have been given but a few breaths in this brief realm called time. How will you use them?

My friend, all too soon—in the twinkling of an eye—your bridegroom will return to take you home. On that glorious day, you will see your Beloved face-to-face and have the answers to every question you have been searching for.

You are known.

You are loved.

You are home.

> "The people who walked in darkness
> have seen a great light;
> those who dwelt in a land of deep darkness,
> on them has light shone."
> —Isaiah 9:2

. . . Behold, I am coming soon.

Two worship songs that beautifully capture the heart of this week's lesson are "Even So, Come (featuring Chris Tomlin)" by Passion and "You Are Beautiful" by Phil Wickham. May they minister to your heart as they have to mine, as you await the blessed return of your King.

> "He will wipe away every tear from their eyes, and death shall be no more,... for the former things have passed away.... 'Behold, I am making all things new....'"
> —Revelation 21:4–5, selected

Notes

[1] These instances do not include passages referring to other persons named Ishmael or any passages referring to "the Ishmaelites" in general.

[2] Unlike the other five names, the author lists Midian as a noun, giving reference to the region and people group that eventually came to be called Midianites.

[3] It appears that the two brothers remained in somewhat close contact, as more than twenty years later, Isaac's son Esau would marry Ishmael's daughter Mahalath, also named Basemath (Gen. 28:9).

[4] The singular expression "gathered to his people" is also used of Aaron (Num. 20:24–26) and Moses (Deut. 32:48–50). A similar expression "slept with his fathers" refers to the death of Israel's various kings, found throughout 1 and 2 Kings and 1 and 2 Chronicles.

[5] J. D. Currid, *A Study Commentary on Genesis*, vol. 1, *Genesis 1:1–25:18* (Darlington, England: Evangelical Press, 2003), 437.

[6] Thomas B. Dozeman, "The Wilderness and Salvation History in the Hagar Story," *Journal of Biblical Literature* 117, no. 1 (1998): 33.

[7] Quoted from Esther 4:14.

[8] The words "raised" and "seated" are written in the Greek verb form called aorist active indicative. The use of the indicative mood by the author means that the author is making a statement of fact.

[9] St. Augustine, *The Confessions of St. Augustine*, bk. 1, sec. 1.

[10] Christ's Bride is clothed in "fine linen"; however, this imagery is in reference to the marriage in heaven. See Revelation 19:7–8.

[11] This is not the same word used in verse 18, when God says, "I will make for him a helper." In that verse, the verb "to make" is *eeseh*, which refers to causing something to be done, accomplished, or established. That verb is used throughout Genesis 1 to describe God making (or causing) the sun, moon, stars, beasts, and livestock to come into existence. It is used again when God says, "Let us make man in our own image." However, the first time the Hebrew verb "to build" appears in Scripture is in Genesis 2:22.

[12] J. Swanson, *Dictionary of Biblical Languages with Semantic Domains: Hebrew*, Old Testament (Oak Harbor, WA: Logos Research Systems, 1997), Logos edition.

[13] Compare Isaiah 60:11, 19–20 with Revelation 21.

[14] Compare Ezekiel 47–48 with Revelation 21–22.

NOTES

ALSO BY

Shadia Hrichi

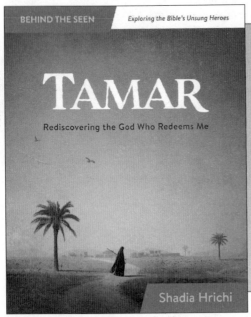

ISBN 978-1-68426-301-1

BEHIND THE SEEN — *Exploring the Bible's Unsung Heroes*

TAMAR

Rediscovering the God Who Redeems Me

Shadia Hrichi

If God can choose the Canaanite Tamar to continue the line through which Christ would come, can anything keep Him from weaving your story into His redemptive plan? Through this six-week in-depth Bible study, you will discover that no matter life's twists or turns or your sins and failures, there is a God redeeming everything for His glory.

"If you enjoy squeezing every delicious drop of truth from the stories found in Scripture, Shadia Hrichi's new study on Tamar will delight you. She handles God's Word with exceeding care, pointing us to the many vital lessons worth learning and applying to our own lives."

—**Liz Curtis-Higgs,** best-selling author, *Bad Girls of the Bible*

ISBN 978-1-68426-370-7

BEHIND THE SEEN — *Exploring the Bible's Unsung Heroes*

LEGION

Rediscovering the God Who Rescues Me

Shadia Hrichi

Experience God's relentless love as you follow the man known only by the name of the demons that tormented him. Through this action-packed, six-week study, rediscover for yourself what it means to have Jesus intercede on your behalf.

"Shadia has written another outstanding study. *Legion* is rich and in-depth. There were so many new insights; several brought tears to my eyes. Well written and well organized, this study is packed with valuable life lessons. I can't wait to read the next one!"

—**Francine Rivers,** international best-selling author

...diahrichi.com for updates on new books ...d resources in the Behind the Seen series.

LEAFWOOD
PUBLISHERS
an imprint of Abilene Christian University Press